CROSSCURRENTS *Modern Critiques*

CROSSCURRENTS *Modern Critiques*

Harry T. Moore, *General Editor*

Minor
British Novelists

EDITED BY *Charles Alva Hoyt*

WITH A PREFACE BY
Harry T. Moore

Carbondale and Edwardsville

SOUTHERN ILLINOIS UNIVERSITY PRESS

FEFFER & SIMONS, INC.

London and Amsterdam

Copyright © 1967 by Southern Illinois University Press
All rights reserved
Library of Congress Catalog Card Number 67–10029
Printed in the United States of America
Designed by Andor Braun

PREFACE

ENGLISH LITERATURE has many mansions, and fortunately it provides special little houses for those residents designated as minor. The present book is an excursion through some of those outlying houses (cottages?), and it is a fascinating excursion. In one way it is like a visit to one of those secondhand bookshops that cling to the edge of university neighborhoods—on dusty back shelves one finds ancient copies of Everyman's Library editions of Mrs. Gaskell, Fanny Burney, or Thomas Love Peacock, with faded gilt titles which promise the book-pilgrim many hours of enrichment.

That English literature is the world's greatest is a point rarely challenged, and there is no need, here, to call the roll of giants who make it so. It is the very existence of so many giants that makes possible the great number of minor authors. Among these, the survivors are often very good, and they frequently have special qualities not found in any except the most nearly universal of the larger authors. Mrs. Gaskell's Cranford, for example, cannot be compared with the achievements of Shakespeare or, say, Dickens, yet Cranford is unique. There is not, of this particular kind, any other picture of English village life, even in Hardy. Cranford has its own distinct atmosphere.

And so do many other books mentioned in this volume, which should prove to be as useful as it is enjoyable. Charles Alva Hoyt had a good idea when he thought of this book, and he has carried it out well, with—it seems in case after case—just the right people to comment on these novelists. For graduate students in English the book will be a blessing, and general readers who wish to know more about the subject will find that the present studies will induce them to read the fiction discussed here, which is eminently worth reading, as all these critics so amply demonstrate. But the reader I most like to think of in connection with this volume is the one who relishes English literature and who knows something about the novelists talked about in these pages—and who will then give the books of those writers a fresh reading.

Not that the present book is merely a beamish appreciation; on the contrary, it is consistently a work of authentic criticism. That is, it evaluates as well as illuminates. The title of the book itself suggests evaluation, or at least the acceptance of an evaluation, for just who are and who are not minor is determined (or at least has been until the present age of critical intensification) by Dr. Johnson's "common reader," who in the course of time overrides or accepts the judgments of the critics and professors. Anyhow, the reader is warned of evaluation by the title of this book; but he will find out for himself how illuminating it is.

Some of the statements made here are not precisely new, but they are necessary to the presentation of these authors. On the other hand, a good deal that is said here is fresh, or at least freshly said. Bernard McCabe's essay on Disraeli is a case in point. Mr. McCabe's examination of the resolution, in Disraeli, of the antipodes of the Romantic and the rational seems to me to contain some valuable observations well worked out. Similarly, Charles Alva Hoyt's remarks on Robert Smith Surtees' use of sporting language show not only how this idiom has cut down response to Surtees among present-day readers but also go on to demonstrate how skillfully Surtees employed such locutions. W. B. Coley conveys to us the "Irish" flavor of Maria

Edgeworth's writings, with some extremely serviceable explorations of their technique as well as their meaning.

Charles Shapiro makes it clear how much better Mrs. Gaskell was when not engaged in special pleading, and Fred B. Millett provides elucidating comments on the nature of talk in the novels of Thomas Love Peacock. Berta Nash gives us new perspectives on Arthur Machen when she emphasizes the important points she has found in The Great Return, not always so highly regarded by Machen's readers. Eugene White's essay on Fanny Burney is both a significant appreciation, explaining why Fanny Burney is so good, and an excellent background-piece to the other essays since it includes some expertly presented historical material as to the early development of the novel as a genre. William J. Lockwood adroitly explains the comic techniques of Rose Macaulay, and Frederick S. Wandall helpfully examines the elements of Christian allegory in the world of Charles Williams.

These are only a few of the features of the present essays, all of which are full of sound information, credible judgment, and significant insight. And note that the critics in this volume don't see these novelists only in relation to authors of the past; observe the references to James Joyce, Sherwood Anderson, F. Scott Fitzgerald, William Faulkner, and other writers of our own time.

In preparing this book, Mr. Hoyt was given a free hand to choose his subjects and commentators. There was no kibitzing or I might have suggested the addition of the man I consider to be the finest among neglected British novelists: Francis Stuart. The ideas he adhered to in the 1930's and 40's were abhorrent, but the novels he has written since the Second World War (perhaps as a kind of atonement) deserve more attention than they have received.

In relation to the present book, I am most happy to renew my association with Professor Emeritus Fred B.

Millett, of whom Mr. Hoyt speaks so nicely in his introduction. Mr. Millett was my teacher at the University of Chicago more than thirty years ago, and I learned much from him that was helpful. He had been trained in Renaissance studies in the days when it was heresy to think of teaching anything "modern," but at Chicago he was a pioneer in contemporary English (and American) studies, and in all ways a brilliant educator. His essay is not alone in its excellence. All the writings in this volume do credit to their authors and make this a most rewarding book. We must be grateful to these critics for this most useful new panorama of minor British novelists.

HARRY T. MOORE

Southern Illinois University
October 12, 1966

CONTENTS

A COLLEAGUE OF MINE has suggested that I find a more prestigious title for this book. I suppose that there must be a critical euphemism for the word "minor," but I am not interested in finding out what it is. Like the little old lady on the quiz show, I prefer a reasonable disproportion to an egalitarianism founded upon sentiment. It was this old lady who, upon being cited by the quizmaster as "seventy-five years young," electrified me and no doubt many others by retorting that she was not young, but old, and that she had thought the fellow had had enough wit to see it.

There is a minor novel, as there is a major novel. The boundaries between them are not always perfectly clear, but the territories remain well separated in the mass. Dostoyevsky is a major novelist; Disraeli is a minor one. And yet I think no one will deny that there are times when a reader will fly from Dostoyevsky to Disraeli, or from George Eliot to Ronald Firbank. Excellence is no property of sheer bulk; and therefore to reassure those who are uneasy about some of the connotations of the word "minor," it may be well to revive here the distinction between "second-rate" and "second-rank." Max Beerbohm, to lead from strength, is the sort of figure one might describe as of the second rank, but there is manifestly nothing second-rate about him.

This brings us to the question of a more meaningful distinction. Among writers of high rank, I believe it is a question of conception and ambition as well as one of ability. Minor novelists are not categorically to be so considered because of deficiencies in their art, but because they conceive of the world in more limited terms than the titans do; they are less ambitious. As Max Beerbohm said of himself, they mark out a comfortable niche and fill it decoratively. I do not wish to suggest that had Mr. Beerbohm wished to, he could have written *Crime and Punishment*. There is involved a fundamental question of volition, as there is in the old schoolboy conundrums about God: could He make an object so big that He Himself couldn't lift it? It takes a certain attitude about God to imagine Him involved in such a business, as it takes a sort of track-meet approach to literature to rank the novelists, with five points going to first in each event, four to second and two each to a third-place tie.

The minor novelist may be, like John Galt, fascinated with a certain locality; or a certain occupation, like Captain Marryat. He may be perfectly content to spend all his energy and art upon a question of theology, like Charles Williams. We have not the right to demand that he apply himself to issues of more widespread significance; as Dr. Johnson observed, no man owes the world any specified amount of poetry.

Of course the major novelist may also be considered in terms of his preoccupations: Hardy and Faulkner are devoted to region, although neither is strictly speaking a regional novelist (Mr. Coley incorporates into his essay an excellent discussion of this question). Trollope is as fond of clergymen as Captain Marryat is of sailors; and Tolstoy, perhaps, is as interested in religion as is Charles Williams. The difference is that in each case the major figure conceives of his preoccupation in terms of the whole world, while the minor can see the world only in terms of his preoccupation.

There is a concession of superiority in that evaluation that may not be avoided, and should not be, but I shall close this portion of my remarks as I began, with the reminder that greatness is not a commodity for all seasons. The perfect antidote to a week of Proust is an evening with Saki. And there are undoubtedly some who would prefer the mixture in inverse proportion.

It remains to introduce the contributors to this volume. The first, Eugene White, is Professor of English at Ohio Wesleyan and an eighteenth-century scholar whose list of publications includes a book on his present topic: *Fanny*

Burney, Novelist: A Study in Technique. W. B. Coley is also a well-known eighteenth-century scholar, the editor of the forthcoming Wesleyan University edition of Fielding. He is Professor of English at Wesleyan University in Middletown, Connecticut.

Fred B. Millett is the Nestor of this volume. Professor Emeritus at Wesleyan University, where he directed the Honors College, he is the author of a large number of studies, especially upon the novel, as well as some of the most successful and challenging textbooks ever conceived. A former president of the American Association of University Professors, he is a man widely known to the profession.

Having successfully, we hope, distinguished between various Wesleyans, we come next to the editor, Charles Alva Hoyt, Associate Professor of English at Bennett College. He is the author of numerous articles, principally upon nineteenth- and twentieth-century figures. His studies and reviews of contemporary fiction have appeared in *Saturday Review, Commonweal, Columbia University Forum,* and the *New York Times Book Review,* as well as in several volumes of the Crosscurrents series. Bernard McCabe of Tufts is another contributor to many publications, most frequently perhaps to *Commonweal.* As will be seen, the fiction of Disraeli has been one of his principal studies.

Charles K. Shapiro is no stranger to the readers of the Crosscurrents series, as this is at least his fourth appearance. He is editor of the volume *Contemporary British Novelists* and author of *Theodore Dreiser: Our Bitter Patriot.* Among the many journals and magazines that regularly present his views of fiction are the *New Republic, Saturday Review,* and *The Nation.* He teaches at Briarcliff College.

Our only woman contributor is Berta Nash, among other things a housewife and mother, but also a sixteenth-century scholar and dabbler in many realms of the curious in literature, particularly bibliographical and Renaissance. She is thus well qualified to deal with Machen in whom she has long been interested. She holds the Ph.D. from Chicago and has taught there and at Louisville and Wayne State universities.

It has been said that one should be a theologian as well

as a literary critic to understand Charles Williams. Such requirements necessarily limit the field severely, but Fred B. Wandall qualifies. A practicing Episcopal priest, graduate of the General Theological Seminary, he has also taught English at the University of Pennsylvania. He holds a Litt.B. from Oxford, where he was a member of Christ Church and Chaplain in the Cathedral. At Oxford his major study was the religious thought of Matthew Arnold, but Williams is an old favorite with him and the subject of his undergraduate thesis.

Finally, Mr. William Lockwood of the Bennett English Department. Mr. Lockwood, a recent graduate with highest honors from Williams College, is a Ph.D. candidate at Pennsylvania, where he is dividing his time between modern fiction and the Renaissance. This is his first published article.

CHARLES ALVA HOYT

Millbrook, New York
March, 1966

Minor British Novelists

FANNY BURNEY

Eugene White

I am sure there's a great deal of human *life* in this book, and of the manners of the present time. It's writ by somebody that knows *the top and the bottom*, the *highest* and *lowest* of mankind—It's very good language, and there's an infinite deal of fun in it.

The book was *Evelina*. The speaker was Mrs. Thrale. And the man to whom she spoke was Dr. Burney, her daughter Queeney's piano teacher and the father of Fanny Burney, a young lady of exceptional modesty and decorum who had done an extraordinarily unconventional thing. She had written surreptitiously and had managed to get published anonymously a novel in a day when it was at best questionable whether a well-brought-up young lady of proper morals should even read such a work.

Now with the fame of the book spreading, with speculation about its authorship enlivening tea-table conversation all over London, and with her beloved father's reaction to having his daughter known as a novelist uncertain, Fanny lived each day in fear of exposure to humiliation and ridicule if not disgrace. But Dr. Burney, his first fears overcome by surprise and delight at the merit of the writing, had made it his business to find out how it was being received by those people whose opinions would in large measure determine the public attitude.

Mrs. Thrale's pronouncement was typical of what

he heard. And what father is going to remain silent long about his daughter's accomplishment in an atmosphere of approval like that? So it was that Evelina Anville and her creator, Fanny Burney, made their "entrance into the world" and helped to shape the direction which the newest of literary forms was to take from that time on.

Some account of the state of the novel when *Evelina* appeared in January of 1778, might be helpful in understanding certain aspects of Miss Burney's contribution. Not a clearly defined genre either in form or purpose, the novel had evolved in the eighteenth century from the escapist French romances and their English imitators, the epistolary stories which for security kept a handhold on the essay while probing experimentally in sometimes dubious directions, the crime stories catering to the insatiable appetite for vicarious experience in the sensational underworld of the rogue, and the short stories called novels appearing separately or within longer works or periodicals. With *Don Quixote* and *Pilgrim's Progress* and the narratives of Defoe serving as landmarks on the way to the true novel—a fiction which sheds light on human life and human emotions in the here and now through the artistic structuring of reality into coherent and meaningful form—Richardson and Fielding and Smollett and Sterne had each in his own way added a dimension to the newly developing genre. They had not completely freed it from the older, traditional forms of literature (if, indeed, it has ever been so freed), but they had given it a recognizable shape that distinguished it as a literary form and had at least indicated something of the limits and the possibilities of that form. And working within these limits and aware of these possibilities, Fanny Burney used her talent for minute and accurate observation of character and manner, and her gift for portraying with charm and affection the life which she saw in all its fascinating variety and incongruity, to fashion works of art which reveal certain refinements and technical improvements linking her as clearly with Jane Austen and the modern novel as with her predecessors.

Most obvious is her originality in dramatizing the ordinary happenings of everyday social life and in making them significant in the development of her conventional plots. This flair for the dramatic, this ability to see in the affairs of the moment the possibilities for revelation of character, for humor, for ludicrous or revealing juxtaposition, for the exposure of affectation and pretense is conspicuous in her early diaries and letters. They abound in scenes which bring to immediate life some incident, some encounter, some character which the observant eye or the quick ear of the quietly self-effacing young girl had stored up for the time when she could escape to her room and commit it to paper. As a result her diaries and letters provide one of the most revealing as well as the most charming records of the life of the times, recreating in vivid detail the social patterns of eighteenth-century England and the forms and manners of the great, the near-great, and the humble in that varied circle in which she moved. The unexpectedness, the singularity, the endless variety to be found in the usual never ceased to fascinate her and to provide material for her pen.

But there is another element involved here too. A great part of the originality in Miss Burney's novels is in the point of view. As G. B. MacCarthy has pointed out in *The Female Pen*, up to this time women had generally been pictured as men see them. Richardson, through his experience in writing letters for young ladies, had come very near achieving the feminine viewpoint. But in *Evelina* it is revealed completely: we see a young girl, not as she appears to men, but as she is herself, shy, ignorant of how to behave, confused, lacking in self-confidence. Miss Burney had written since childhood for her own amusement, and consequently she wrote from her own point of view about the things in ordinary life and society which interested her and ordinary young women like her. It is perhaps understandable then that a novel which took the commonplace and presented it aesthetically so that it was somehow made new while still wonderfully familiar should have its appeal to the young ladies who were patrons of the circulating libraries. Miss Burney expected no less. What she did not expect was that men like Edmund Burke, Edward Gibbon, Joshua Reynolds, Richard Brinsley Sheridan, Dr. Johnson—and Dr. Burney—would find it equally fascinating. That they did is evidence of a quality in the work which is shared by all true works of literature: a concern with reality.

Limited by her sex, by her position in society, by what the customs of the time decreed proper for a young lady to see and hear, Miss Burney still was observant enough and imaginative enough to see within that perspective the reality which Lionel Trilling has cited as the essential concern of all literature. In his discussion of "Manners, Morals, and the Novel," he says that this concern is with the opposition between what really is and what merely seems. The field of research for the novel is always the social world, the material of its analysis being always manners as the indication of the direction of man's soul. The novel, he says, is born in response to snobbery— that is, pride in status without pride in function, a pride that asks, "Do I belong . . . ? And does he belong? And if I am observed talking to him, will it make me seem to belong or not to belong?" The purpose of the novel is to record this illusion born of snobbery and to attempt to penetrate to the truth hidden beneath all the false appearances. This preoccupation with appearances and with the truth behind them is the very heart of Miss Burney's works. And it is a central preoccupation of man as a social being, whether male or female, schoolgirl or literary critic.

No important novelist, of course, transfers material

from life directly to his pages, even if such a thing were possible: he selects and recombines and sharpens his material in order to give it meaning and dramatic power. In his selecting, coloring, and intensifying of experience he takes the vague, illogical, half-perceived apprehensions and reactions to life which obscure its meaning and presents them vividly and with a simplified coherence. He focuses attention on essentials.

Miss Burney's success rests largely upon her ability to place herself in the situation she is describing and to sense what her characters must feel. It is, in fact, in achieving what she stated explicitly to be her purpose in her Preface to *Evelina:* "To draw characters from nature, though not from life, and to mark the manners of the times. . . ." And to achieve this goal she chose to introduce "upon the great and busy stage of life" a young lady "with a virtuous mind, a cultivated understanding, and a feeling heart" whose "ignorance of the forms, and inexperience in the manners of the world, occasion all the little incidents which these volumes record."

Working then from surface appearances, from the external forms which her characters presented to society, Miss Burney was adept at finding the distinguishing traits, the idiosyncrasies or unique qualities that marked them as individuals. But she knew human nature well enough to know that the real person could be discovered only on longer acquaintance. She also knew that it is in our reactions to the unusual or unexpected that we are most likely to show what we are. Our guard is down, our prepared responses are inadequate. The essential part of her character-drawing thus lies in providing occasions for the characters to show reactions from which the reader can form judgments. From the accumulating judgments he gains his complete conception of the characters. Miss Burney was wise enough to let her characters speak for themselves and to leave the process of judgment, for the most part, up to the reader.

But at the same time she recognized the value to be gained from the indirect method of showing the effect which a character's actions and words produce on others. In many of her scenes, and often in preparation for a dramatic scene in which a character will reveal himself in action, the attitude of other characters helps us to form at least a tentative judgment which can be tested and confirmed or modified in the subsequent action. This indirect method of character revelation has become popular since Miss Burney's time, but she seems to be among the first to recognize its usefulness.

Certainly in the revelation of character one of Miss Burney's great talents lay in her handling of dialogue. She had a good ear for the patterns and rhythms of speech. She had trained it well as she listened to the lively give and take among the varied guests who appeared at the concerts in the Burney home. Italian opera stars, actors (including the close family friend David Garrick who amused the children by his take-offs on other guests), clergymen, authors, painters, politicians, lords and ladies, cousins and aunts, even the Russian Prince Orloff: the list is astounding. And they all found their way into Fanny's diary, speaking in their very tongues. In her anecdotes and character sketches she made them speak in character and reveal much of themselves in what they said and how they said it. When she came to her created characters in the novels, her talent was ready at hand. And one indication of her success in using it is the fact that fashionable literary London was soon amusing itself by repeating the characteristic tags and clichés of the humorous characters in *Evelina*.

The speech of her characters is differentiated as it had not previously been done in the novel. Each character speaks the idiom of his segment of society consistently. The language is no doubt a fairly accurate reproduction of the speech of the time as Miss Burney heard it and recorded it for amusement and future use. But each character also speaks in such a way as to identify him as a person within his group, an individual who is unlike all the others in important ways. Through his speech as well as through his actions he reveals to us what he is.

Another principle of technique which she found useful to her purpose was that of broadening her social scene by letting each of her characters represent to some extent a whole segment of society. Thus she was able to give the illusion of a many-faceted social background with its varied structure and texture without the overcrowding which might in fact tend to nullify such an effect. She does it by suggestion, by leading the reader to fill in around the typical characters others of their type to make the scene complete.

And she groups her characters for contrast. Indeed, her first attempt to write a novel grew out of her curiosity to see what would happen if people from different levels of society were brought together: what possibilities for fun, for testing of values, for ridiculing of affectation, for pointing up the merits of propriety and good taste, of sincerity and good humor, might be found in such a juxtaposition. Let us hasten to observe that this is not the snobbish sport of an In-group ridiculing the gaucherie of the Outs. Miss Burney was well aware that virtue and vice, sincerity and pretense, taste and tastelessness are not clearly divided between the Ins and Outs. She did not confuse manners and morals. She did not equate social position and moral worth. She judged actions by the motives which inspired them. She related happenings to meanings in her search for reality, for a valid picture of what is worthwhile in a world of seeming.

The impression received from reading a novel like *Evelina*, then, is a conviction of reality. This surely is the fashionable London of the late eighteenth century. This is the way its people looked and acted and thought. This is the tone of its society. And this is the variety that existed within that society, the range and scope within the little world which contained, as Dr. Johnson said, all of life within its narrow bounds.

This is to imply that setting is important in Miss Burney's works, as indeed it is. For the first time in the English novel setting has become essentially functional. But it is a social setting, not the external world of nature and things which plays such an artistic and symbolic part in the novels of Conrad and Hardy, but the details of London life which she develops not as simply a backdrop for her dramatic scenes, but as causative factors in shaping the action. Her characters are what they are in large measure because of the social environment of which they are a part; they act as they do because of the various demands and expectations of that environment; and the course of the plotted action in the total work is shaped largely by the interplay of character and setting. It is Evelina's introduction into a new and unfamiliar setting that brings about all the incidents which compose the history of her entrance into the world. It is the pulling of a character or a group of characters from its own part of the social setting into one with a different set of manners and with different modes of thinking that provides much of the humor and the testing of values in the course of the consequent action. It is the adaptation to the larger setting and the searching through its outward forms to its core of meaning that constitutes the ethical progress of the story. Plot, character, and setting function aesthetically as dependent parts of a total structure. One cannot be divorced from the others.

It is evident, then, that Miss Burney worked with considerable sophistication in developing an artistic form which was solidly based on the best of what had been done and which brought something of its own in the way of refinement and direction. Mrs. Thrale's judgment of *Evelina* that "there's a great deal of human life in this book" has a validity that needs to be recognized as fully as that of the rest of her sentence:

"and of the manners of the present time." The manners strike us today as perhaps the most notable and
enjoyable aspect of the book. But the manners are the
medium through which Miss Burney portrays life in
its deeper and more meaningful aspects. In developing
a surface that pleases and delights, she has not been
remiss in attention to that twin classical precept that a
work of art must also instruct. And what she teaches is
a concern for the feelings of others, a benevolent attitude, humility, sensitivity, sincerity; the shunning of
affectation, extravagance, and frivolity; an appreciation of the rich texture of everyday social life and a
good-humored enjoyment of its ludicrous moments.

Her sensibility marks her a woman of her time. Her
ability to recognize the limits beyond which it became
vanity marks her a woman of good sense. She was
sentimental in something of the way in which Lau-
rence Sterne interprets the term in the work which she
called one of her favorites, his *A Sentimental Journey*.
It is a sentimentality able to distinguish between surface polish which results in courteous actions and a
politesse de coeur which leads to humane ones. Let us
have sentiment, he would say to us, but sentiment
rightly founded on a sympathy for others which arises
out of an understanding of them gained only by understanding ourselves. Let us have romance—the
world is a dull enough place without the added dis-
coloration of the jaundiced eye—but let us not assert
that the truth of romance is all of the truth. Let us
recognize the posturings of others by recognizing our
own, and find the truth of human nature in the delightful contrasts to be found only when we do not
disdain or fear "to walk up a dark entry" where "in
such an unobserved corner you sometimes see a single
short scene . . . worth all the sentiments of a dozen
French plays compounded together." And having
found this truth, let us cherish the affections which
rise out of it and "love each other—and the world,
better than we do."

Fanny Burney's sentiment was of this high order. She does not hold with the crowd of lesser writers who seem to say that feeling is to be cultivated for its own sake and that the more tears we can coax out the better persons we become or prove ourselves to be. Like Sterne, she speaks for the receptive heart, the sympathetic searching into human motivations which engages our sensibilities and unites us with others in bonds of understanding and affection. But her sense of decorum and the satiric quality of her humor, which made her keenly aware of the ridiculous, kept her from the excesses of sentiment which overflow much of the writing of the time.

I like Fanny Burney. I like her Pride and her Prejudice. I like her Sense and her Sensibility. I like her humor, her gentleness, her charm. I like her because she was a person and not just a personality. I like her diaries and letters and her four novels: *Evelina, Cecilia, Camilla,* and *The Wanderer.* I am not so unrealistic as to believe that in this day of vastly expanding knowledge when courses in speed reading are necessary to help us keep up with the news many people are going to read them. But many people might and undoubtedly will do worse than to read at least the diaries and *Evelina.* They bring to life in a way no other works that I know of do a people and a time which have profoundly influenced our own and which still have something to say to us which I think we ought to hear.

AN EARLY "IRISH" NOVELIST

W. B. Coley

IN AN AGE nurtured on books like *The Naked Lunch* and made anxious by smooth statements of apocalypse, it is not the easiest job in the world to make the case for a novelist like Maria Edgeworth. Indeed it may be difficult to make the case for many of the novelists comprehended by the present volume. Who needs *minor* novelists? And British minor novelists, to boot? In its basic form, at least, the question is an ancient one, and the answers to it are themselves so ancient and various that they can hardly be rehearsed here. At issue is the parochial tendency of the most recent thinking about literature to become more and more antihistorical, even ahistorical. Literary criticism appears to be in revolt against notions of literature as some sort of autotelic activity. In the practise of the so-called new critics these notions were themselves often charged with being insufficiently alert to the findings of historical scholarship. But the ahistoricism, if any, of the new critics is as nothing compared to that of the apocalyptic school, with its emphasis on self-revelation, social action, commitment, and other strong assertions of the proximity of the literary act to the continuum of felt life. A decade or so ago one of the senior contributors to this volume was asked to join a group discussion of the nature and aims of literary study. He refused politely, stating that the only reason for studying literature was the enjoyment that came from reading books. Today, who is seriously content to rest his case on this mild form of the pleasure principle? Has there ever been an age when readers read so much in terms of self, so therapeutically? Perhaps. Somewhere. But not recently. For most of us today the historical orientation is pointless. The past, if present at all, is present only to be disavowed.

Should the foregoing sketch be even superficially fair, it will suggest how prejudiced must be the case for Maria Edgeworth, for her case today is to a considerable degree historical. Someone has said that Jane Austen was a better novelist but that Miss Edgeworth was the more important. Whatever we may think of the evaluation, we should ponder the distinction. Important in what way? To the history of the novel in English, of course. Not that Miss Edgeworth is not worth reading in or for herself. Simply that she is also worth reading because she contributed significantly to the process of enlargement and change which came over the novel in English between its eighteenth-century manifestations and the great Victorian accomplishments. In literary history as elsewhere the question of who was the first to do a particular thing is a hard one to answer and possibly not so important as historians tend to make it. It compels us to be extremely careful about definitions, for one thing. If we are careful, we can make a claim for Maria Edgeworth as the first "Irish" novelist, which is to make her the pioneer of a tradition which later includes, if it does not culminate in, A Portrait of the Artist as a Young Man and Ulysses. There are other reasons, even other historical reasons, for attending to Miss Edgeworth, but this reason will do for a start. To explain how the first "Irish" novel came to be written by an Oxfordshire spinster who did not settle in Ireland until she was fifteen requires a rehearsal of some of the anomalies with which Miss Edgeworth and her subject territory were liberally surrounded.

Maria Edgeworth (1767—1849) was born at Black Bourton, Oxfordshire, the second child of the first legitimized marriage (of four) of Richard Lovell Edgeworth. Her mother died when the novelist-to-be-was six years old and although her father, who was something of a lady-killer, married again in the same year, he perforce became an extraordinary influence on his daughter's personality and career. Not that Edgeworth would have been noticeably less influential had the first Mrs. Edgeworth survived, for he was an extraordinary man in his own right. Born at Bath in the year of Pope's death (1744), of a family that had been settled in Ireland since the sixteenth century, he underwent an education that was as Anglo-Irish as his background. He was said to have dissipated his time at Trinity College, Dublin, and to have spent it more purposively at Oxford, where he married the first Mrs. Edgeworth while he was still an undergraduate. He seems to have emerged from his education as almost a parody of that familiar eighteenth-century type, the eccentric rationalist philosopher with a strong interest in science, in practical science in fact, and a strong political conservatism. An inveterate projector of a kind that would have been still recognizable to Swift, Edgewworth propounded educational theories in the spirit of Rousseau, patented a number of mechanical inventions (including a kind of telegraph), became a fellow of the Royal Society, was friends with Wedgwood, Humphry Davy, Ann Seward, and Erasmus Darwin, managed to bore Byron, and was regarded by some as the father of modern road making. In politics and social administration Edgeworth was a meliorist. In 1782 he left England to return to the hereditary estate in County Longford with the aim of improving it, superintending the education of his numerous progeny (there were to be over twenty), and contributing to the betterment of Ireland. As will be seen from the running title of his daughter's first novel, the year 1782 was significant in more ways than one. The

Edgeworths arrived in Ireland to find that Grattan, with the Protestant Ascendancy mobilized behind him, was extracting from London what amounted to a concession of Ireland's right of self-government. "Ireland," Grattan is supposed to have said, "is now a nation." He was in error, of course. The nation was hopelessly divided on such matters as Catholic emancipation, the need for land reform, and the political system of rotten boroughs. "Great hatred, little room," Yeats would call it later. Edgeworth seems to have sensed it even then and went away from Dublin north some sixty miles to his estate at Edgeworthstown to effect "the melioration of the inhabitants." Almost at once he made changes. Traditionally Irish landowners made use of bailiffs or middlemen to manage the renting apparatus and relations with the tenants. Traditionally these middlemen, like Chaucer's reeve, were reputed to milk the system by abusing their relationship to both parties. Edgeworth dispensed with their services, abolished the feudal dues and the idea of duty work and payment, and insisted that all rents be paid directly to him. What is more, he implicated his entire family in the system by requiring that all of them understand both the rationale and the procedures of his modified system. Maria, in particular, he made his estate agent and general secretary.

At first glance Maria Edgeworth could not have appeared to possess the qualities requisite for such a position. Plain in appearance, almost dwarfish in stature (she lacked five inches of being five feet tall), educated in female academies and à la Rousseau at home, she must have inherited some of her father's anomalous streak of practicality, for the position of estate agent was an onerous one and all the evidence suggests she filled it well. What the whole experience —it extended over many years—did for her fiction is incalculable. It may account for the absence of a characteristically feminine sensibility in most of her novels, which differ markedly from those of Jane Austen, for example, in that the casual reader would not be certain to attribute them to a woman. More probably her managerial experience accounts for the relatively wide scope of the world of her fiction. To adapt a famous remark made in another connection, she found the novel made of marble and she left it made of brick. That is, as an eighteenth-century lady novelist she inherited the novel of manners and broke out of it, in her "Irish" works at least, to establish a wider range of fiction than had been attempted up to that time. Scott's big bowwow she may not have had, but she did more than engrave finely on a piece of ivory with Jane Austen. When the Wolf Tone-inspired and French-assisted uprising of 1798 wrote finis to Grattan's dream and nearly brought down the Edgeworth estate about its owners' ears, Maria Edgeworth, or so it is pleasant to imagine, may have been hard at work in the Edgworthstown drawing room getting on with what has been called "the brilliant requiem of the Protestant Nation." Two years later (1800), the year the Act of Union legislated out of existence what Burke had called "a natural, cheerful alliance" with England, there appeared in London and then in Dublin the first edition of *Castle Rackrent: An Hibernian Tale taken from Facts and from the Manners of the Irish Squires, before the Year* 1782. Published anonymously, it was the first complete novel by Maria Edgeworth.

As its running title clearly implies, *Castle Rackrent* is in some ways more like a tale than like what today would be recognized as a full-fledged novel. It is short. It is narrated or told by a person. And it has considerable affinity for what in American literature would be called the tall tale. Furthermore, the flavor of the book is extremely anecdotal. In her Preface Miss Edgeworth takes some pains to defend what she saw as a prevailing public taste for anecdote. She supports such a taste against the tony critical charges that it was trivial and low and in doing so links the fact of anecdote to the much larger issue of verisimilitude in literature. The novel, we see clearly today, has always had an interesting, if shifting, relationship to history. From the very beginning the claims of fiction to deal with the real world have been measured, often invidiously, against those of its supposedly more literal sister activity. Unlike poetry, in its modern phases at least, the novel has had to contend with the problem of realism on many fronts. The novel's bulk, its very prosaicness, its slowness, these and other characteristics have somehow made the genre more vulnerable to charges that it was not getting at reality. We have only to review the eighteenth-century precursors of Miss Edgeworth to see how often their novels masquerade as Lives, Histories, Histories of Lives, and the like. As her own preface makes clear, to write fiction was to write history. History of a very special sort, to be sure, for in her view most professional or public historians wrote impossibly fanciful and inflated history. She argues that the best, the most genuinely instructive history takes the form of secret memoirs, private anecdotes, familiar letters, the careless, even unfinished conversations of domestic, not public, life. Her preference for documents like these seems to have had two important corollaries for her larger view of fiction itself. First, she believed in collecting the "most minute facts relative to the domestic lives, not only of the great and good, but even of the worthless and insignificant." Minuteness and particularity were not exactly staples of most eighteenth-century novels, as we hardly need Dr. Johns 's streaky tulip to remind us. Nor are they exactly taples of *Castle Rackrent,* as it turns out, for the very brevity of that work precludes the sort of density of detail which marks and sometimes disfigures her later work. On the other hand, the relatively few "facts" which *Castle Rackrent* supplies are indeed minute in the sense of trivial and informal and domestic. And these characteristics remind us of Miss Edgeworth's notion that the novel as history ought to turn away from the public and pompous toward the private and simple, toward what the sensibility of a later day would call "the little person." As the professional historian can hardly be bothered with the private circumstances even of public figures, to say nothing of the private circumstances of the poor and unimportant, it is to the biographer that we must turn for the truth that lies behind the scenes.

A second corollary of Miss Edgeworth's view of the proper business of the historian-biographer is that the latter succeeds in inverse proportion to the extent that he intellectualizes or makes literary his productions. "A plain unvarnished tale is preferable to the most highly ornamented narrative." An antirhetorical doctrine this, a call for simplicity. And in *Castle Rackrent* the call is heeded. Miss Edgeworth goes through all the old business of pretending that the book is in fact the memoirs of "an illiterate old steward" of the family that owned the castle. Like Defoe, Swift, and a raft of her lesser predecessors, she pretends the publication of the book is owing to an editor, whose function it is to write down the narrator's account and to provide the ignorant English reader with explanatory notes and glossings of difficult Irish terms. In these somewhat technical respects *Castle Rackrent* is well within the familiar conventions of fiction. Less conventional, however, is the placement of the narrator within the book. In eighteenth-century narrative fiction the tendency was to put the narrator in the center of his narrative, that is, to make him the narrator of his own life or his own experiences. Moll Flanders and Lemuel Gulliver, for example, function as autobiographers. On the other hand, Thady Quirk, the illiterate narrator of *Castle Rackrent*, tells the story not of his own life but of the family which he was born and bred to serve. He functions as both a participant and an observer and in this sense is more like Nick Carra-

way of *The Great Gatsby* than he is like Lemuel
Gulliver. There is at least one important gain for
fiction in this more sophisticated handling of the narrator. No longer need the reader's view of things be
utterly dependent on and exactly coextensive with the
narrator's view of things. We depend to a considerable degree upon what Thady Quirk discloses, but our
final estimate of the meaning of his disclosures must
also take into account the fact that it is Thady who is
making the disclosures. That there is a problem of
perspective here which is missing in most earlier fiction can be demonstrated by comparing the sometimes binocular effects of *Castle Rackrent* with the
unremitting flatness of the narrative in *Moll Flanders*.

Perhaps Miss Edgeworth's most celebrated contribution to the history of the novel is her creation of
what can be called a genuinely *regional* locale. *Castle
Rackrent* has in fact been called the first regional
novel in English, a statement which, though it may
raise all the old doubts about questions of primacy,
deserves to be pondered. Until Edgeworth and Scott
the novel in English was not much interested in region as such. For one thing, neoclassical aesthetics did
not encourage the treatment of place in so detailed
and specific a way as to make regional effects possible.
Fielding may have composed *Tom Jones* with the aid
of a map and an almanac, but whatever new verisimilitude this may have effected was largely topographi-
cal. Erase the place names in Fielding and you have
no idea where you are. *Humphry Clinker*, to take one
more case, undertakes to describe Scotland and the
Scots, especially Edinburgh and its people, but it
would be an act of the sheerest partiality to argue that
Smollett thereby created much of a sense of region.
Ireland, one might retort, cries out for regional treatment. Perhaps. But where in the considerable Ango-
Irish literature of the seventeenth and eighteenth centuries do we find it so treated? Gothic novels have
often been cited for their contribution to fiction's

sense of setting, but the setting of a Gothic novel depends for its effect on an absence of any recognizable resemblance to real places living or dead. Therefore, perhaps Miss Edgeworth's primacy in this respect has merit. Scott at least thought so. In the postscript to *Waverley* (1814), which has itself been called the first *historical* novel, he speaks of having drawn inspiration from the Irish portraits in the work of Miss Edgeworth.

At this point it seems sensible to make a tentative distinction between the regional novel and the historical novel, between, that is, Miss Edgeworth and Scott. Properly speaking, the regional novel does two things which are vital to any conception of it. First, it creates a sense of reciprocity between persons and places such that we no longer see the isolated stage Irishman, for example, that buffoon of farce, but an aggregate of persons living together in some sort of distinct society or culture. This society or cultural grouping ought to give us a genuinely autochthonous sense of having sprung from the very ground or region it is described as inhabiting, taking on the coloration of its habitat, so to speak, and in turn effecting certain changes in that habitat by virtue of certain characteristics acquired from it. Fielding describes Joseph Andrews as an *autokopros*, literally, sprung from a dunghill, but no one has ever seriously maintained that Joseph was therefore a regional type. Fielding does not bother to establish any integral relation between the hero and the specifics of his habitat. Joseph in fact transcends his dunghill and thereby transcends geography and region. For Miss Edgeworth, however, the dunghill makes a difference. It produces distinctive offspring known as Irish, and these in turn treat their dunghill in a way that is distinctive and Irish. Which leads us to the second thing the regional novel must do. It must create a region or a world that is recognizably like some region or part of the nonfictional world. Ireland, for example, or Wessex, or the American

Middle West, or Yoknapatawpha county. It is this second requirement of the definition which excludes the Gothic novel from taking its place with the regional novel.

The historical novel would appear to derive, at least in part, from the regional novel, in that it too requires the capacity to present a world identifiable in both place and time, a society with characteristics that are more than merely the reiteration of certain type characters inhabiting it. This capacity the historical novel could have found already suggestively employed in the regional novels of Miss Edgeworth, as Scott amiably asserted he had found it in *Castle Rackrent*. In *Waverley*, of course, Scott gives us more than just a study of a society or of a world. He retrieves a time sufficiently remote or seemingly remote from his own that it can be called a historical time. And he endows it, though vanished, with the same kind of plausibility that the regional novelist achieved for certain pockets of a world which, although not literally contemporary, does not quite strike us as past either. Time in the sense of pastness, then, is one of Scott's contributions to what he found already available; and history, too, in the sense of a notion of causality, the interdependence of events previously seen either as timeless or as merely having sequence. Neither of these two concepts—pastness and history—seems quite to have been within Miss Edgeworth's grasp as a writer. Although *Castle Rackrent* contains several editorial assertions that it deals with "other times," that the manners it represents are "not those of the present age," the objective reader may well feel that pastness is not achieved by such assertions or by claiming that the fictional date of the work is 1782. And yet, Miss Edgeworth's common theme is the effect of the past upon the present, particularly as manifested in lingering and ineffective traditions or ingrained cultural habits. Still, a backward look of twenty years or so is nothing to the nineteenth-century novelist. So short a backward look tests fully neither the precision of the novelist's historical memory nor his powers of wholesale retrieval of what he has remembered. And to treat the past as present in the present is really not the same thing as making a plausible reconstruction of a bygone era. To be sure, Miss Edgeworth is more acutely aware of the past and its effects than, say, Fielding. When Fielding credits the lawyer in *Joseph Andrews* with having been alive "these four thousand years," he is choosing to be ahistorical, to cut his character off from normal space-time, to universalize him, as it were. In *Castle Rackrent*, at least, Miss Edgeworth does no such thing. Her characters seem clearly located in both time and place. It is simply that compared to Scott's, they strike us as insufficiently past.

The assertion is sometimes made that the historical novel must deal with great public (i.e., historical) events. To put it another way, this kind of novel must establish a serious interrelation between the fictional and the historical events that take place in it. If we apply such a criterion rigorously, we cannot call *Castle Rackrent* a historical novel. As she made clear in her Preface, Miss Edgeworth held little brief for the historian who dealt in public events or historical occasions. She thus takes her place in that great shift in the attitude of the novel toward the private and the trivial, so brilliantly elucidated in Auerbach's *Mimesis*. On the other hand, by all but excluding recognizable historical occasions from her book she may have prevented herself from accomplishing the historical novel. Our imagination doubtless warms to think of her hard at work on her requiem of the Protestant Ascendancy while the Rising of 1798 eddied about her very doors, but the hard fact is that in Thady Quirk's narrative there is scarcely a whisper about the background of Irish history. One can retort that it takes more than the mere presence or absence of historical events to make or break, as it were, a historical novel. Part of *Tom Jones*, for example, takes place against the specific background of the Scottish rebellion of 1745. Yet there is a world of difference between Fielding's treatment of the Forty-five and Scott's. In *Tom Jones* the Forty-five bears about the same relation to the events played off against it as the topography or meteorology of Tom's journey to London bears to the events of that journey. The relation in these cases is more or less a matter of plausibility, of verisimilitude. In Scott's *Waverley*, on the other hand, the Forty-five is shown to be in some sense both a cause and an effect of the events Scott chooses to write about. Today we should call such a relationship "organic," and we would probably not consider that Miss Edgeworth had quite got it. However, to harp thus on her supposed defects is to insist that she be a kind of novelist she in fact is not. Perhaps we would do better to sum up her historical importance by reminding ourselves that she did much to prepare the way for Scott and possibly Turgenev, to teach the nations in their greater name, as it were, and thus can be said to have helped change the sensibility of an age, a function not given to many to perform.

There are of course other, more immediate reasons for reading Miss Edgeworth today. *Castle Rackrent*, for example, is a book capable of pleasing still. Thady Quirk, its illiterate narrator, is moved by affection for the now vanished family of Rackrents to recount his memories of four generations of its principal members. Rackrent was not in fact the family's original name. Sir Patrick O'Shaughlin took the name as a condition of inheriting the Rackrent estates upon the death without issue of Tallyhoo Rackrent, a cousin-german, who died, as his name almost tells us, in a hunting accident. The extinction of the direct Rackrent line is an early hint of the frailty of the aristocratic ideal, particularly as the basis for organizing a modern society, and it becomes the implicit aim of the novel to demonstrate this frailty in all its forms. Sir Patrick was what we should call today a party boy. His parties were so good, in fact, that gentry came from miles around, even in the dead of winter, to partake of the convivialities. As Thady recounts this early part of his tale, he is apparently seated opposite a portrait of Sir Patrick, whom he never saw in the flesh. The way he uses the portrait to bring the departed squire to life is masterful.

> he must have been a portly gentleman—his neck some-thing short, and remarkable for the largest pimple on his nose, which, by his particular desire, is still extant in his picture—said to be a striking likeness, though taken when young.—He is said also to have been the inventor of raspberry whiskey, which is very likely, as nobody has ever appeared to dispute it with him, and as there still exists a broken punch-bowl at Castle-Stopgap, in the garret, with an inscription to that effect—a great curios-ity.

Sir Patrick dies, in a brief, brilliant scene, after cele-brating his birthday with his drinking friends. His going out, like his coming in, was a fine affair, marred only by the fact that as the hearse was passing through his own town, the body was seized for nonpayment of debt.

Sir Murtagh Rackrent, the heir, turned this insult to the dead into a brilliant ploy. With the backing of his fellow gentry, he refused, as a point of honor, to pay off his father's debts: "the moment the law was taken of him, there was an end of honor to be sure." This is the first outright confrontation between the squirearchy and the class which was eventually to un-seat it, the somewhat amorphous middle class of es-tate agents, professional men, and those in trade. For a time Sir Murtagh appeared to be beating them at their own game. Totally unlike his father, he put an abrupt end to conviviality and the open house. Tight-fisted to the point of rapacity, he married rather suit-ably into the great Skinflint estate, taking as his bride a lady every bit as close with money. However, like his predecessors, Sir Murtagh had his problem, his essential flaw, though it wasn't drink. Obsessively litigious, he had, or claimed to have, a lawsuit for every letter in the alphabet. At one time sixteen were running concurrently, and his office, according to Thady, was so crammed with legal papers one could hardly turn around in it. Sir Murtagh may have won more suits than he lost, but even those he won cost him "a power of money" and he was forced to sell off "some hundreds a year of the family estate." Perhaps it might have turned out all right in the end—he had a great case on against the Nugents of Carrickashaughlin— but against Thady's advice he dug up a fairy mound so as to utilize the ground, and things went bad. The end came in a passionate dispute with his lady over her share of the renting income. At the height of his passion Sir Murtagh ruptured a blood vessel and died, whereupon Lady Rackrent, being childless, "took herself away to the great joy of the tenantry," and the estate went to her husband's younger brother, Sir Kit.

Sir Kit's tenure began badly. A spendthrift young army officer, he tired of the place after the hunting season was over and so put it into the hands of an agent, "one of your middle men, who grind the face of the poor," and betook himself to Bath. The agent ground the tenants in the approved way and enlisted the services of Thady Quirk's son Jason as a clerk and accountant. With the appearance of Jason Quirk the modern reader may well sit up and take notice, for the anticipation of Flem Snopes, Faulkner's famous creation, is absolutely stunning. Like Flem, Jason begins his career unobtrusively as a clerk in what might be called the commercial hub of his region. At first Jason would take nothing at all for his trouble, being "always proud to serve the family." The next we hear of him, however, he has managed to put in for a good farm which had recently fallen into his master's estate. With Sir Kit an absentee and Thady himself letting it be known in the country that "nobody need bid against us," Jason got his farm and set the pattern of his career. It was but a matter of time before Sir Kit, increasingly encumbered with gambling debts and the expenses of fast living, fell out with his agent over money and transferred his accounts into Jason's hands. This crisis evidently stirred Sir Kit into attempting to make good the defects of his income by the most conventional of means. He married a rich and sophisticated Jew whom he had met at Bath and brought her back to live on his estate. She abhorred Irish life and when she refused to surrender her money and jewels to his management, Sir Kit locked her up in her room for seven years, taking her meals in to her himself and allowing not another soul to catch a glimpse of her. At length she had "a sort of fit" and, the country assuming her dead, several ladies whose affections Sir Kit had been trifling with demanded he make good his promises to them. In an ensuing duel he was shot dead and his wife was then released from her captivity to return to England and civilization.

From this point onward the novel pursues something of a double track, recounting the rise of Jason Quirk and the fall of the House of Rackrent, the two careers being intimately connected. Sir Condy Rackrent, the new and final heir, is so brilliant a feat of fictional imagination that his fortunes must not be recounted here. Enormously popular with all strata of society, unpremeditating to a fault, he committed a whole series of memorably pointless acts: flipping a coin to decide between his heart and his head in marriage, staging a mock-funeral so that he might be a spectator at his own obsequies, dying while attempting to win a bet that he could drink off a great horn full of liquor without drawing breath. Against his pointless, poignant charm and indomitable good nature Miss Edgeworth sets the Snopes-like purposiveness of Jason (now Attorney) Quirk as he nears his golden fleece. This final section of *Castle Rackrent* is well worth comparing to the first book of Faulkner's trilogy on the Snopes family, *The Hamlet*. Not only is Jason a striking prefiguration of Flem Snopes, but the treatment of Ireland is very similar to Faulkner's treatment of the South. The same sense of the land is in both books, the same sense of region. The attractive yet debilitating effect of the presence of the past in the present modulates, in both cases, to a sense of foreboding, of defeat, of curse upon the land. The gradual deterioration of the Rackrent estate under the maladministration of its owners finds its corollary in Varner's Frenchman's Bend or Hubert Beauchamp's Warwick. Both Faulkner and Miss Edgeworth make use of the tall story, the anecdote, the remembered tale. Even their narrator figures resemble one another. V. K. Ratliff, the sewing machine agent in *The Hamlet*, does not in fact narrate the story directly as does Thady, but he discharges narrative functions in other ways and, what is more, he resembles Thady in a number of personal characteristics, not least in his mixed attitude toward the new man, Flem Snopes.

The preceding, rather sketchy comparison of *Castle Rackrent* and *The Hamlet* is offered, not so much as evidence that Faulkner must have read Miss Edgeworth at some time or other, as an encouragement to the modern reader to read the earlier work. Although it is without question the most immediately accessible of her novels, *Castle Rackrent* is by no means Miss Edgeworth's only triumph. It is not even her only "Irish" novel. Readers who have yielded to its charm and accomplishment will want to turn to *The Absentee* (1812) and *Ormond* (1817) for more on the Irish scene. These are much bigger books than *Castle Rackrent* and much less triumphantly placed and unified by tone and teller. One hesitates whether to attribute such defects to the intrusive hand of Richard Lovell Edgeworth—absent from *Castle Rackrent* but present in nearly everything else—or to Miss Edgeworth's superior abilities in the short form. The defects are perhaps only relative and are by no means crucial. The broader canvas brings with it great advantages as well. *The Absentee*, which Ruskin said was a better guide to Irish politics than all the gazettes put together, gives detailed treatment to a situation comprehended only briefly in *Castle Rackrent* by the early tenure of Sir Kit: the network of social abuses created by a system of absentee ownership which permitted the gentry to luxuriate irresponsibly in England while back on the land the tenants were being squeezed to make such luxury possible. Ruskin's remark may be compared with one attributed to a historian of more recent vintage, to the effect that *Middlemarch* gives us the best extant social history of England on the eve of the Reform Bill. Not every reader fancies himself as a social historian, of course, or is even much interested in the historical aspects of fiction. We must remind ourselves, therefore, that there are other reasons for reading *Middlemarch*, as there are other reasons for reading *The Absentee*. In Lady Clonbrony the latter novel has one of Miss Edgeworth's great achievements in character. We may not be much in the habit of judging today's fiction in terms of character, but it is a perfectly suitable way of judging nineteenth-century fiction. In addition, *The Absentee* tackles a magnificent theme, namely, the problem of personal and national identity in the face of the fact that Ireland no longer existed as a nation. The hero, Lord Colambre, tries to answer the question of his personal and national identity by returning to Ireland, where he finds his estates brutalized and corrupted by the mismanagements of the Jason Quirk types. The spectacle so stirs him that he decides to remain in residence and "meliorate" the tenants. This solution is hardly a satisfying one. Indeed it may have taken its form from the determinations of Richard Lovell Edgeworth, who seemed to think that to deal with Ireland as either a modern political entity or an ancient feudal mythology was out of the question. Miss Edgeworth may not have thought her solution very satisfying either, for she makes one last attempt at the problem in her last novel of Irish life, *Ormond*, published in the year of her father's death (1817) and showing signs of his intrusive hand. The eponymous hero, who has been called an Edgeworthian Tom Jones, is raised as an orphan and given the opportunity to decide which of Ireland's three faces he wishes to turn toward: the Anglo-Irish landed gentry, the political governors of the Protestant Ascendancy, or the ancient feudalities of the proscribed and outlaw Catholic families. Ormond begins, naturally enough, by admiring the last. And as the novel presents this "face" in the character of "King Corny" O'Shane, it is not hard to see why. "King Corny" is a masterpiece and the mythic attractions of his life are compelling. But the O'Shanes, like the Rackrents, are a fated lot; their glamor and their poignancy are somehow pointless. As he matures, Ormond begins to switch his allegiance toward Sir Herbert Annaly, the resident Anglo-Irish landowner, who resembles nothing so much as an awkwardly fictionalized Richard Lovell Edgeworth. Once again the solution seems somehow tepid and unsatisfying, but Miss Edgeworth modifies it a little by having Ormond surround himself with mementoes of the "old" Ireland and her feudal vigor. It is her last word on the "Irish problem."

There is, it must be noted, one other Edgeworth novel worthy of mention here, the novel of manners entitled *Belinda* (1801). Jane Austen admired it as displaying "the greatest powers of mind . . . the most thorough knowledge of human nature," and anything Jane Austen praises so highly we should attend to. *Belinda* is a London, not an Irish, novel, and in stretches it reads like almost any of a number of novels of manners in the years after Burney. Like much of Miss Edgeworth's fiction, it is redeemed in large measure by the presence of a great character. Lady Delacour, the brilliant leader of the London *haut monde* into which the heroine is thrust, is an almost Proustian invention. At war with herself, contemptuous of her society, by her own account "a strange, weak, inconsistent figure," she suffers from cancer of the breast and conceals it from the world, a symbol of the concealed sickness of her society. When Lady Delacour dominates *Belinda,* the book is brilliant. The very fact that Miss Edgeworth could create a living character so remote from her own attitudes and concerns testifies to her range and might remind us also how professional, in one sense, the art of fiction has become, how few of even our serious novelists today have what might be called the amateur's audacity to extend their range. Miss Edgeworth made substantial contributions to the literature of education and pedagogy; she was a writer of children' stories that were read for generations and served as models for the genre; she has been called the first novelist to take seriously the working of the economic system and to put this concern into fiction. But if she had done none of these things, the "great Maria," as Scott called her, would be worth reading as just a novelist.

Castle Rackrent is a genuine masterpiece. To have read it is to have taken a step or two, an irretrievable step or two, into a fascinating world of fiction.

THOMAS LOVE PEACOCK

Fred B. Millett

STUDENTS OF ENGLISH LITERATURE may remember that
Thomas Love Peacock was the author of an essay,
"The Four Ages of Poetry," which inspired Percy
Bysshe Shelley to write the most eloquent of statements of romantic literary theory, his "Defence of
Poetry." The ideas Peacock expressed in this semi-
serious essay furnish us a clue to the view of life that
underlies the novels that concern us here. He found it
impossible to accept the idea that the progress of
civilization is inevitable; instead, he maintained that,
through the centuries, civilization had slowly deterio-
rated. He distinguished four ages: the iron or bardic,
the golden, the silver, and the brazen. He felt that the
age in which he was living was the age of brass, and
that its materialism and scientism were unpropitious
for the production or consumption of poetry. Students of the romantic period in English literature may
recall that, surprisingly enough, the authors of the
opposed theories expressed in these essays were close
friends. Extraordinarily diverse in temperament, they
managed to achieve a loyal and devoted friendship.
They met when Peacock was twenty-eight and Shelley
was nineteen. Shelley described Peacock as an "amiable man of great learning, considerable taste, an en-
emy of every shape of tyranny and superstitious im-
posture." At various periods during Shelley's brief life,
they saw each other frequently, and, when Shelley and

Mary Godwin went to Italy in 1816, Shelley wrote a remarkable series of letters to Peacock describing their travels. Although Peacock was a staunch defender of Shelley's first wife, the unfortunate Harriet West-brook, and felt less enthusiasm for Mary Godwin, he was sufficiently devoted to Shelley to manage to be on fairly good terms with all the persons in this famous triangle. For a time, Shelley gave Peacock an annuity. Peacock assisted in the management of Shelley's affairs after he settled in Italy. Shelley made Peacock one of the co-executers of his estate and bequeathed him two thousand pounds. Peacock's *Memoirs of Percy Bysshe Shelley* is one of the major authorities on Shelley's early life. Peacock's novels, however, are so idiosyncratic that they are likely to be known only to close students of the history of the English novel and to the few members of each generation of readers who belong to the Peacock cult.

The life of Thomas Love Peacock was, as he would have wished it, relatively uneventful. He was born on October 18, 1785. His father, Samuel Peacock, was a glass-merchant. His mother was the daughter of Thomas Love, who had been the master of a man-of-war. Samuel Peacock died when his son was three years old, and the mother and child went to live with her father at Chertsey on the Thames. The mother was well educated, is said to have been a regular reader of Gibbon, and contributed a great deal to her son's education. He did, however, attend a day school be-tween the age of six and thirteen. At the end of that time, he and his mother moved to London. Although for a brief period later he worked in a business office, he devoted himself to continuing his education by reading at the British Museum, became one of the best classical scholars of his day, and acquired an inti-mate knowledge not only of Greek and Latin but of French and Italian literature. He spent the winter of 1808–9 as private secretary to Sir Home Popham, commander of the fleet in the Downs, but found

himself in a "floating inferne" that was unpropitious
for writing or the continuation of his education. During the next year, he travelled in Wales and fell in
love with Jane Gryffydh, but evidently felt that his
prospects did not permit him to press his suit.

By 1819, when he was thirty-four, his financial situation had worsened and he entered the office of the
East India Company. Surprisingly enough, he proved
to be a valuable company man and finally succeeded
James Mill, the father of John Stuart Mill, as exam-
iner at a salary of two thousand pounds a year. It
was Peacock who recommended the use of steam ves-
sels to carry the mails monthly to India, which had
been receiving mail from England only twice a year. It
is not necessary to take too seriously his light verses
about the working hours at India House.

> From ten to eleven, ate a breakfast for seven:
> From eleven to noon, to begin 'twas too soon;
> From twelve to one, asked, "What's to be done?"
> From one to two, found nothing to do;
> From two to three began to foresee
> That from three to four would be a damned bore.

Within a year after entering India House, he wrote a
very business-like letter to Jane Gryffydh, proposing
matrimony. She accepted and they were married in
1820. In 1823, he bought a cottage for himself and his
wife at Lower Halliford on the Thames and an adjoining cottage for his mother. Her death in 1833 was a
great shock to him, and this shock, along with his
official responsibilities, may account for the fact that
he did not write or publish another novel for twenty-
five years after her death.

Peacock's domestic life was made unhappy by his
wife's semi-invalidism and the failure of his eldest
daughter's marriage to the impecunious young novelist, George Meredith. Peacock retired from India
House in 1856, when he was seventy-one and passed
the rest of his life at Lower Halliford, reading, walk-

ing, boating, and playing with his grandchildren. He spent most of his time in his beloved library and allowed no one, except his granddaughter Edith, to enter it. There, at the age of seventy-three, he wrote his last novel, *Gryll Grange*. Peacock had a morbid fear of fire, and, when his house caught fire, he refused to leave his library. "By the immortal gods," he shouted, "I will not move." The shock of the fire, however, seems to have been too much for him, and he died on January 23, 1866.

Critics of Peacock have argued as to whether he was a Conservative or a Radical. The truth of the matter would seem to be that he was of too independent a mind to adhere to either political philosophy without qualification. Peacock's way of thought exemplifies admirably the Greek ideal of "nothing too much," the Aristotelian golden mean. His hostility to extravagance in any form led him to attack conservatism when it was too conservative and liberalism when it was too liberal. It is certain, however, that he viewed with extreme distaste many of the innovations that were changing the society of his time. He was hostile to the machine, to universal education, to paper money, to the science of political economy, and to Scotchmen. He was, in the popular sense of the term, an Epicurean. His ideal was tranquillity, and he devoted himself to the pleasures of tranquillity: reading, walking, the company of his close friends, dining, and consuming Madeira.

It took a considerable amount of experimentation in literary forms before Peacock discovered one in which he could say effectively what he wanted to say. He wrote and published a good deal of poetry, but his more serious poems are too full of what Wordsworth castigated as "poetic diction" to have much to offer modern readers. He is at his best in the numerous songs and ballad-like poems that adorn his novels. In his early years, he had hopes of being a writer of comedies, but he abandoned that hope. He was, however, sufficiently shrewd to make use of some of the themes and characters of his comedies in the form of the novel that he was to make his own.

Peacock's characteristic novels are more or less elaborate variations on the same pattern, one that, in the history of English fiction, he made indubitably his own. So eccentric are these characteristic novels that no critic has been able to hit upon an altogether satisfactory description of them. One writer has called them Platonic dialogues, caricatured by Aristophanes, and Peacock's admiration for Aristophanes and his imitation of him in "Aristophanes in London" in *Gryll Grange* give some support to this notion. J. B. Priestley has called them "novels of talk." I suggest the parallel phrase, conversational novels.

The form of Peacock's novels remains fairly constant. The setting is usually the country house of a somewhat eccentric gentleman of independent means. His passion for hospitality encourages him to invite what Richard Garnett called "a conglomeration of oddities" to what we should call a house party and what the English would call an extended weekend. The minimal plot in Peacock's novels is furnished by one or two love stories treated rather casually and inconsequentially. Furthermore, Peacock is not very much interested in creating full-bodied characters, although sometimes he seems to have a success beyond his intentions. In the main, however, the incidents in the novels are those inevitable to house parties: elaborate meals with plenty of potations, walks in the extensive grounds of the country house, love-making, and entertainments such as sports, cards, dances, the traditional celebration of such a holiday as Christmas, and incessant conversation.

J. B. Priestley has pointed out that Peacock's characters, such as they are, fall into three categories. The first includes the personification of crotchets, the development of a character around some obsessive preoccupation, as Dr. Cranium's devotion to phrenology and Mr. Milestone's passion for formal gardens in *Headlong Hall*. The second category consists of more or less broad caricatures of contemporary persons, and one of the interests of the reader is the identification of such famous persons as Shelley, Byron, Coleridge, Southey, and other less familiar Peacock contemporaries. To the third category belong the inevitable lovers. In them Peacock does not usually show any very intense interest, although occasionally he invests them with a considerable amount of charm, as in the cases of Marionetta and "Stella" (Celinda) and Scythrop Glowry in *Nightmare Abbey* or Lady Clarinda, Sussanah Touchandgo, and Captain Fitzchrome in *Crochet Castle*. But these lovers are as sexless and almost as casual in the disposition of their love affairs as the lovers in a Gilbert and Sullivan operetta, with which, as George Saintsbury pointed out, they have a distinct analogy.

But Peacock's major concern is talk, and his novels are primarily devoted to arguments that range over all the topics that interested him and his contemporaries. Carl Van Doren observed that in *Headlong Hall* the talk embraces such subjects as "the blessings of civilization, the excellence of primitive man, landscape gardening, vegetarianism, the principles of the picturesque, the disposition of literary people, periodical criticism, human disinterestedness, phrenology, alcoholic potation, child labour, the introduction of machinery, the right of might, physical deterioration, dancing, formal society, the relations of music and poetry, and the advantages of matrimony." The talk here does not range more widely than it does in his other novels in this genre. Peacock had a great gift for dialogue, a gift that he may have developed in the unsuccessful comedies he wrote early in life. In Peacock's gallery of talkers, there are no stumblers, no stutterers; he endowed all his upper-class characters with wit and elegance, point and rhythm. But his gift is not limited to upper-class dialogue. He is equally

successful with the speech of such lower-class characters as the sexton in this novel and the delightful rural
lover, Harry Hedgerow, in *Gryll Grange*. Peacock is
also effective in his descriptions of setting, which gave
his particular variety of romanticism an outlet. Devo-
tees of Peacock are very likely to be admirers of a style
that is in essence lucid, classical, French, rather than
English.

Headlong Hall (1816) is Peacock's trial flight not
only in the novel but in the type of novel that he was
to make his own. The novel draws its ideational material freely from the discussions among the frequenters
of the Shelley circle, which both Peacock and Shelley's first wife, Harriet, found distinctly amusing. If
one looks for Shelley among the characters in this
novel, he is probably Mr. Foster, the perfectibilian.
The characteristics of all Peacock's five novels of this
type are present here. The later novels differ from this
one in an increase in subtlety in the handling of his
characteristic devices, a progressive richness of characterization, and a growing freedom in conversational
exposition and argumentation. Here we have the
country house, its owner, the extended house party
composed of guests representing widely different interests and opinion, and a love story treated with high-
handed casualness. The major "philosophers" in this
novel are, as Peacock barefacedly tells the reader,
"Mr. Foster, the perfectibilian, Mr. Escot, the deterio-
rationist, and Mr. Jenkinson, the statu-quo-ite." The
gaucherie of Peacock here is his immediate identification of the view of life of each of his philosophers and,
as the novel goes on, the mechanical presentation of
their views on whatever subject comes up for discussion. At their first appearance, Mr. Foster says, "In
short, everything we look on attests the progress of
mankind in all the arts of life, and demonstrates their
gradual advancement towards a state of unlimited perfection." To this, Mr. Escot replies, "These improvements, as you call them, appear to me only so many

links in the great chain of corruption, which will soon fetter the whole human race in irreparable slavery and incurable wretchedness." Of this utter disagreement, Mr. Jenkinson always takes the middle view. "There is not in the human race a tendency either to moral perfectibility or deterioration; but . . . the quantities of each are so exactly and perpetually *in statu quo*." It is probably through the mask of Mr. Escot that one hears the voice of Peacock himself. "The mass of mankind is composed of beasts of burdon, mere clods, and tools of their superiors. By enlarging and complicating their machines, you degrade, not exalt, the human beings you employ to direct them. . . . All singleness of character is lost. . . . We divide men into herds like cattle: an individual man, if you strip him of all that is extraneous to himself, is the most wretched and contemptible creature on the face of the earth."

In addition to these philosophers, Peacock gives us his first clergyman, The Reverend Dr. Gaster, a very slight sketch for the rounded characters of the clergy in the later novels; Mr. Panscope, who has taken all knowledge for his province and who is a very broad caricature of Coleridge; and Mr. Cranium, the phrenologist, who gives a lecture on his science and one of whose best remarks is "The organ of self-love is prodigiously developed in the greater number of subjects that have fallen under my observation." It is Marmaduke Milestone, in whom Peacock satirizes his contemporary aestheticians who preferred man-made to natural beauty, who is the cause of the most amusing, if farcical, scene in the novel. He persuades the Squire that the prospect of his tower will be improved by "blowing up a part of the rock with gunpowder, laying on a quantity of fine mould, and covering the whole with an elegant stratum of turf." The Squire furnishes the needed materials eagerly. The explosion takes place, but the shock of it precipitates Mr. Cranium from the top of the tower to the waters below. The Squire is chiefly concerned as to the amount of water the victim has consumed, since he has a mortal fear of water. For it, Madeira is the only reliable counteractive, with the result that, after dinner that night, three or four servants were required to carry Mr. Cranium to his bed, since "every organ in his brain was in a complete state of revolution."

Of Peacock's three longer novels, *Melincourt, Crochet Castle,* and *Gryll Grange, Melincourt* (1817) is generally considered the least successful. Most critics feel that it is too long and that some of the discussions become tedious. H. F. B. Brett-Smith, who, with C. E. Jones, edited the Halliford Edition of Peacock's works, surmised that Peacock's publisher insisted that he extend the novel to fit the popular three-volume form, and David Garnett feels that the action subsequent to the abduction of the heroine by Lord Anophel Achthar adds nothing of interest to the story. Carl Van Doren suggested that one of the reasons for the lack of critical enthusiasm for the novel is the fact that many of the subjects considered were of merely topical interest: "rotten boroughs, the irresponsible use of paper money, slavery in the West Indies, Malthusian principles of population, the night of German transcendentalism, the humanity of our simian kin."

Certainly one of the reasons for the comparative inferiority of the novel is the insipidity of the lovers: Anthelia Melincourt and Sylvan Forester, the recluse who has renounced the world but is won back by his not too aggressive love for the heroine. The tone of the heroine, Anthelia, may be caught from this portion of her extended description of an ideal mate: "I would require him to be . . . the friend of the friendless, the champion of the feeble, the firm opponent of the powerful oppressor—not to be enervated by luxury, nor corrupted by avarice, nor intimidated by tyranny, nor enthralled by superstition—more desirous to distribute wealth than to possess it, to disseminate liberty than to appropriate power, to cheer the heart of sorrow than to dazzle the eyes of folly." To Forester, Peacock has attributed his own hostility to slavery, which expressed itself in his refusal to use sugar, and he makes Forester the founder of the Anti-Saccharine Society. He also makes Forester the mouthpiece for his disapprobation of university education, which may have had its roots in the circumstance that Peacock did not or could not attend a university. Forester says of Sir Telegraph Paxarett: "I have great hopes of him. He had some learning when he went to college; but he was cured of it before he came away. Great, indeed, must be the zeal for improvement which an academical education cannot extinguish."

A far more unusual character than the lovers is Sir Oran Haut-ton, the strong silent hero of the tale. The idea for this character Peacock derived from the eccentric Lord Monboddo, whose views he quotes at length in his footnotes and who maintained that the orangutan is a class of the human species and that its want of speech is merely accidental. But, as Richard Garnett pointed out, the idea "does not admit of extensive development; we have soon extracted all that is to be had from it," despite the fact that his heroic actions enliven the book considerably. One of the most brilliant comic scenes in the novel, indeed, is the political contest for the rotten borough of Onevote where the candidates are Simon Sarcastic and Sir Oran. The latter, of course, does not make a speech, but Mr. Sarcastic makes up for him by expounding his code with unabashed boldness. "The constitution says that no man shall be taxed but by his own consent: a very plausible theory, gentlemen, but not reducible to practice. Who will apply a lancet to his own arm, and bleed himself? Very few, you acknowledge. Who then, *a fortiori*, would apply a lancet to his own pocket, and draw off what is dearer to him than his blood—his money? Fewer still of course: I humbly opine, none.—What then remains but to appoint a royal college of state surgeons, who may operate on the patient according to their views of his case?"

The most enduring interest in *Melincourt* is the extraneous one of the caricatures of well-known persons of the period. Mr. Fax obviously represents Malthus; indeed, a paraphrase of his theory is put in Mr. Fax's mouth: "The cause of all the evils of human society is single, obvious, reducible to the most exact mathematical calculation. . . . The cause is the tendency of population to increase beyond the means of subsistence." It is Mr. Fax who creates one of the best comic scenes in the novel when at the church door he attempts to dissuade a rustic couple from matrimony, a scene that gives Peacock a chance to show his skill in handling characters from lower-class life. In the character of Mr. Mystic, Peacock satirizes Coleridge far more tellingly than he did in Mr. Panscope in *Headlong Hall*. The visit to Cimmerian Lodge, Mr. Mystic's home, is capital, if broad, satire. Other Lake poets also receive attention for, although Peacock admired their poetry, he abominated the conservatism to which they turned in their later years. Here his chief butt is Robert Southey, who appears as Mr. Feathernest, who "had burned his old 'Odes to Truth and Liberty,' and had published a volume of Panegyrical Addresses 'to all the crowned heads of Europe,' with the motto, 'Whatever is at court is right.'" Even Wordsworth is presented as Peter Paul Paperstamp, Esq., who is "chiefly remarkable for an affected infantine lisp in his speech, and for always wearing waistcoats of a duffel gray."

Nightmare Abbey (1818), critics generally agree, is the best of Peacock's shorter novels. Its unity is achieved by its single purpose. As Peacock wrote Shelley, its purpose was "to bring to a sort of philosophical focus a few of the morbidities of modern literature and to let in a little daylight on its atrabilarious complexion." The object of its satire is the darker phase of romanticism, of which the Byron of *Childe Harold* was the spokesman. The crude romanticism of the English Gothic novel and the imported Germanic horrors had given way, as Mr. Flosky (Coleridge) points out, to what Peacock regarded as a more dangerous manifestation of the romantic spirit. "The ghosts have therefore been laid, and the devil has been cast into outer darkness, and now the delight of our spirits is to dwell on all the vices and blackest passions of our nature, tricked out in a masquerade dress of heroism and disappointed benevolence." With this phase of romanticism, Mr. Flosky is sympathetic, and he speaks of a tragedy on which he is engaged, in which there is a "dashing young man, disinherited for his romantic generosity, and full of the most amiable hatred of the world, and his own country in particular, and of a most enlightened and chivalrous affection for himself. Then, with the addition of a wild girl to fall in love with him, and a series of adventures in which they break all the Ten Commandments in succession . . . , I have as amiable a pair of tragic characters as ever issued from that new region of belles lettres, which I have called the Morbid Anatomy of Black Bile." Mr. Flosky represents German transcendentalism, which Peacock links with the variety of romanticism of which he disapproved. "I pity the man," Mr. Flosky says, "who can see the connection of his own ideas. Still more do I pity him, the connection of whose ideas any other person can see. . . . Now the enthusiasm for abstract truth is an exceedingly fine thing, as long as the truth, which is the object of the enthusiasm, is so completely abstract as to be altogether out of the reach of the human faculties."

But the particular object of Peacock's satire is Byron, who is introduced briefly as Mr. Cypress, and who justifies his desertion of his country by saying, "Sir, I have quarreled with my wife, and a man who has quarreled with his wife is absolved from all duty to his country. I have written an ode to tell the people as much, and they may take it as they list." Mr. Cypress expounds his pessimism in a paraphrase of some

stanzas from *Childe Harold*: "Our life is a false nature: it is not in the harmony of things; it is an all-
blasting upas, whose root is earth and whose leaves are
the skies which rain their poison-dews down upon
mankind. We wither from our youth; we gasp with
unslaked thirst for unattainable good; lured from the
first to the last by phantoms—love, fame, ambition,
avarice—all idle and all ill—one meteor of many
names, that vanishes in the smoke of death." The lyric
Mr. Cypress sings is better than many of Byron's own
songs.

> *There is a fever of the spirit,*
>   *The brand of Cain's unresting doom,*
> *Which in the lone dark souls that bear it*
>   *Glows like the lamp in Tullia's tomb:*
> *Unlike that lamp, its subtle fire*
>   *Burns, blasts, consumes its cell, the heart,*
> *Till, one by one, hope, joy, desire,*
>   *Like dreams of shadowy smoke depart.*
>
> *When hope, love, life itself, are only*
>   *Dust—spectral memories—dead and cold—*
> *The unfed fire burns bright and lonely,*
>   *Like that undying lamp of old:*
> *And by that drear illumination,*
>   *Till time its clay-built home has rent,*
> *Thought broods on feeling's desolation—*
>   *The soul is its own monument.*

That Bryon did not resent this portrait is evident in
that he sent Peacock a single rosebud which Peacock
preserved until his death.

Peacock rather improbably assigns some of his criticism of Byronic misanthropy to one of the novel's
eccentrics, Mr. Asterias, an ichthyologist, whose object in life is to discover a mermaid. He contrasts such
misanthropy with the kind of Epicureanism that Peacock himself exemplified. "A gloomy brow and a tragi-
cal voice seem to have been of late the characteristics
of fashionable manners: and a morbid, withering,

deadly, antisocial sirocco, loaded with moral and political despair, breathes through all the groves and valleys of the modern Parnassus." But for the wise man, "Nature is his great and inexhaustible treasure. His days are too short for his enjoyment: *ennui* is a stranger to his door. At peace with the world and with his own mind, he suffices to himself, makes all around him happy, and the close of his pleasing and beneficial existence is the evening of a beautiful day." But Mr. Hilary is also Peacock's spokesman when he astutely suggests the source of Byronic misanthropy. "Misanthropy is sometimes the product of disappointed benevolence; but it is more frequently the offspring of overweening and mortified vanity, quarrelling with the world for not being better treated than it deserves."

But the central figure in *Nightmare Abbey* is neither Mr. Cypress (Byron) nor Mr. Flosky (Coleridge) but Scythrop Glowry (Shelley). Scythrop has renounced the world and sunk into despair because of an unhappy love affair; at the same time, he has ardent hopes for the reformation of mankind. He has written a treatise, *Philosophical Gas, or a Project for the General Illumination of the Human Mind,* which has been greeted with less enthusiasm than he had hoped. Scythrop's despair, however, is lightened by his response to the charms of his cousin, Marionetta Celestina O'Carroll, who tantalizes him by seeming to blow hot and cold in her feelings for him. His relations with her are complicated by his interest in a mysterious young woman who calls herself Stella, asks him to protect her, and whom he lodges secretly in the tower to which he withdraws in his more melancholy moments. In the climax of the novel, he discovers that Stella is really Celinda the runaway daughter of the pessimistic Mr. Too-bad. The two women confront each other in an angry scene. "Scythrop knew not what to do. He could not attempt to conciliate one without irreparably offending the other; and he was so fond of both, that the idea of depriving himself for ever of the society of either was intolerable to him." After their immediate departure from Nightmare Abbey, he decides that, if either one will accept him, he will marry her, and, if neither will accept him, he will commit suicide. But, when a letter from Stella (Celinda) informs him that she has become Mrs. Flosky and a letter from Marionetta informs him that she has become the wife of the Honorable Mr. Listless, an extremely lackadaisical young nobleman, he in turn abandons the idea of suicide when he is informed by his tactful butler that the clock by which he was timing his suicide is an hour fast, and, in true Peacockian fashion, consoles himself by ordering Madeira.

In Italy, Shelley had been following the progress of the novel with lively interest and, when the novel reached him, he wrote, "I am delighted with *Nightmare Abbey*. I think Scythrop a character admirably conceived and executed; and I know not how to praise sufficiently the lightness, chastity, and strength of the language of the whole. It perhaps exceeds all your works in this. The catastrophe is excellent. I suppose the moral is contained in what Falstaff says: 'For God's sake, talk like a man of this world'; and yet, looking deeper into it, is not the misdirected enthusiasm of Scythrop what J. C. calls 'the salt of the earth'?" Later, Shelley was to call his study in Italy "Scythrop's Tower." Although neither Shelley nor Mary acknowledged the parallel between the Scythrop —Marionetta—Celinda relationship and the Shelley—Harriet—Mary relationship, they were aware of Peacock's greater enthusiasm for Harriet than for Mary, and there seems little doubt that the triangle in the novel had its source in the triangle in Shelley's life.

In the 1820's, Peacock published *Maid Marion* (1822) and *The Misfortunes of Elphin* (1829), in which the settings were mediaeval and the tone was a curious, but on the whole successful, blend of romance and satire. It may be surmised that, having published three conversational novels, Peacock felt it judicious to attempt fiction in another mode. Of *Maid Marion,* Peacock wrote Shelley, "I am writing a comic romance of the Twelfth Century, which I shall make the vehicle of much oblique satire of all the oppressions that are done under the sun." Although Richard Garnett discovered numerous anachronisms in *Maid Marion,* Peacock was not intent on writing a historical novel in the manner of Sir Walter Scott, whose extremely popular novels he disliked. His researches in Robin Hood literature were not exhaustive. He was content to read Joseph Ritson's *Robin Hood, a collection of all the ancient poems, songs, and ballads now extant relative to that celebrated outlaw* (1795) and the extracts that Ritson printed from Munday and Chettle's Robin Hood plays. "This journey back in the past," as J. B. Priestley has said, "presented the satirist in him . . . with new opportunities. He discovered the trick of satirizing the present in terms of the past, and satirizing the past in terms of the present." Thus, in pointing out the disadvantages of the twelfth century as compared to the nineteenth, he was actually implying ironically that the disadvantages were really advantages.

Maid Marion is primarily attractive for the charm with which Peacock has invested the life in the greenwood, to which all the major characters resort when they are persecuted by the evil Prince John and in which they remain after Robin Hood has been pardoned by King Richard. Richard Garnett pointed out that the novel concentrates "the love of sylvan nature fostered by years of open air life and perpetual rambles in Windsor Forest and by the banks of the Thames." Its tone is reminiscent of Shakespeare's Forest of Arden, the denizens of which "fleet the time carelessly as they did in the golden world." One of the most attractive features of the novel is the interruption of the action by numerous songs, especially those sung by the best of the characters, Friar Tuck. Indeed,

the whole book has an operatic air, and it is not to be
wondered at that it was turned into an operetta by
J. R. Planché, and produced in 1822 under the title,
Maid Marion, or the Huntress of Arlingford, with no
less an actor than Charles Kemble in the role of the
Friar. With judicious excisions, *Maid Marion* might
very well serve as a highly literate version of Robin
Hood stories for juvenile readers.

The Misfortunes of Elphin (1829) is a more considerable work. Peacock had fallen in love with Wales
on his first travels there, but his interest in it was
probably intensified by the fact that in 1820 he married Jane Gryffydh, who was Welsh and well acquainted with traditional Welsh literature. The subject also gave Peacock a chance to indulge his passion
for languages, in this case a new and strange one.
Peacock's chief sources, David Garnett has pointed
out, were *The Myvyrian Archaiology of Wales*, which
was mostly in Welsh, and articles in *The Cambro-
Briton*, a monthly which began publication in 1819.
The Misfortunes of Elphin is Peacock's most complexly plotted novel. In it, Peacock combines the traditional stories about the bard Taleisin and Elphin
and gives them an Arthurian background not in their
originals. The complications arise from the imprison-
ment of Elphin by King Maelgon and the abduction
of Queen Gwenyvar by King Melvas. The bard, Taleisin, who is in love with Elphin's daughter, is the agent
for their rescue. The chief attractions of the novel are
the unfamiliar exotic Welsh material, the brilliant
description of the sea in its wilder moments, the numerous songs which he re-worked freely from the
Welsh originals, notably, the satirical "War-song of
Dinas Vawr," and the character of Prince Seithenyn. It
is his responsibility to guard the Embankment which
protects King Gwyntho's kingdom from the sea, but
he is so addicted to potation that the Embankment
deteriorates and a great flood inundates Gwyntho's
kingdom. Seithenyn is apparently drowned in his

drunken attempt to fight back the sea with his sword, but later it comes to light that two empty wine kegs saved him, and he becomes the butler, first to King Melvas, and later, for his aid in freeing Gwenyvar, second butler to King Arthur. Seithenyn believes that a strong drink will solve life's problems. His motto is "Wine from Gold." J. B. Priestley and David Garnett agree that he is one of literature's immortal drunkards. But Seithenyn is also Peacock's medium for satirizing stubborn Conservatism, of which the spokesman was George Canning, who served briefly as Prime Minister and who has recently been characterized as the most gifted politician of his time. What Peacock disliked was Canning's opposition to any change in the British Constitution. This dislike he expressed satirically in Seithenyn's speech: "Decay is one thing, and danger is another. Every thing that is old must decay. That the embankment is old, I am free to confess; that it is somewhat rotten in parts, I will not altogether deny; that it is any the worse for that, I do most sturdily gainsay . . . Our ancestors were wiser than we: they built in their wisdom; and if we should be so rash as to try to mend it, we should only mar it. . . . There is nothing so dangerous as innovation."

After Peacock's excursion into comic mediaeval romance, he returned in *Crochet Castle* (1831) to the fictive form that he had invented, the conversational novel. There is fairly general critical agreement that, of Peacock's longer novels in this mode, *Crochet Castle* is the best. David Garnett, however, feels that a serious defect of the novel is the unattractive character of the Crochets. The owner of Crochet Castle is a retired Scottish stockbroker, born Ebenezer Mac Crochet, but "he was desirous to obliterate alike the Hebrew and Caledonian vestiges in his name, and signed himself E. M. Crochet, which by degrees induced the majority of his neighbors to think his name was Edward Matthew." The daughter, Lemma, is completely colorless, and the son, Crochet, Jr. who turns out to be a crooked businessman, is not much more vivid. But other critics have admired Peacock's most fully realized clergyman, Dr. Folliott, the two nicely contrasted heroines, Lady Clarinda and Susannah Touchandgo, and such minor characters as Mr. Chainmail, the devotee of things mediaeval, and Mac Quedy, the Scottish political economist. Another attraction of the novel is the change of scene from Crochet Castle to Wales, to which the major characters travel, and Chainmail Hall, with its self-conscious mediaevalism. The conversation, also, has the stylistic qualities that J. B. Priestley has pointed out. "All his people, in spite of individual differences, . . . talk in the same way, like members of a closely united family. They all talk in crisp phrases, delicately balanced and full of antithesis, and with a precision that is at once admirable and droll. However wild their opinions and arguments may be, their actual statements of them are all given an epigrammatic brevity and ring. . . . They explain themselves, as it were, only too well: there is mockery in the very precision of their language and the crisp rhythm of their phrases."

The two heroines of *Crochet Castle*, Lady Clarinda and Susannah Touchandgo are more elaborately characterized than the contrasted heroines of *Nightmare Abbey*. To Lady Clarinda, whom Captain Fitzchrome, who loves her, describes as "the beautiful, the accomplished, the witty, the fascinating, the tormenting Lady Clarinda," Peacock has given more wit than to any of his other heroines; she might have stepped out of a Restoration comedy. She has an air of worldliness that for a time conceals the dictates of her heart. She is at her best in her characterizations of the male guests at Crochet Castle. Mac Quedy, the political economist, she says, is "the Modern Athenian, who lays down the law about every thing, and therefore may be taken to understand every thing. He turns all the affairs of this world into questions of buying and selling. . . . He has satisfied me that I am a commodity in the market, and that I ought to set myself at a high price." Of Mr. Chainmail, she says, "He is fond of old poetry, and is something of a poet himself. He is deep in monkish literature, and holds that the best state of society was that of the twelfth century, when nothing was going forward but fighting, feasting, and prayer, which he says are the three great purposes for which man was made." She is under no illusions about Crochet, Jr. whom her father wishes her to marry; she is perfectly clearheaded about her reason for considering marrying him. "If I take him, it will be to please my father, and to have a town and country-house, and plenty of servants, and a carriage and an opera-box, and make some of my acquaintance who have married for love, or for rank, or for anything but money, die for envy of my jewels. You do not think I would take him for himself. Why he is very smooth and spruce, so far as his dress goes; but as to his face, he looks as if he had tumbled headlong into a volcano, and been thrown up again, among the cinders."

The almost Wordsworthian romantic element in Peacock is most manifest in his characterization of the prosaically named Susannah Touchandgo. After her father's spectacular failure in business and his flight to America, she takes refuge in Wales and lives a simple, devoted life among the peasantry. As she writes to her father, "I have come into Wales, and am boarding with a farmer and his wife. Their stock of English is very small, but I managed to agree with them; and they have four of the sweetest children I ever saw, to whom I teach all I know, and I manage to pick up some Welsh. I have puzzled out a little song, which I think very pretty; I have translated it into English, and I send it you, with the original air." The description of Mr. Chainmail's discovery of her asleep in a tree above a river is perhaps the best romantic scene in all Peacock's fiction. It is no wonder that her charms counteract his desire to espouse a damsel of ancient lineage.

Peacock introduces his best character in *Crochet*

Castle, Dr. Folliott, as "a gentleman endowed with a tolerable stock of learning, an interminable swallow, and an indefatigable pair of lungs." This vigorous character is the mask through which Peacock expresses the aspect of his nature that Priestley calls "the Tory, Greek-loving, Epicurean, anti-reform, unromantic side." Dr. Folliott's first speech expresses Peacock's disapprobation of the politician, Lord Brougham, whose enthusiasm for popular education led to his founding the Society for the Diffusion of Useful Knowledge in 1825 and whose irresponsible conduct when he was Lord Chancellor Peacock thought disgraceful. "God bless my soul, sir!" exclaimed the Reverend Doctor Folliott, bursting one fine May morning into the breakfast room at Crochet Castle, "I am out of all patience with this march of mind. Here has my house been nearly burned down, by my cook taking it into her head to study hydrostatics, in a sixpenny tract, published by the Steam Intellect Society, and written by a learned friend who is for doing all the world's business as well as his own, and is equally well qualified to handle every branch of knowledge." Peacock makes Dr. Folliott the mouthpiece for his own passion for books. "There is nothing more fit to be looked at than the outside of a book. It is, as I may say, from repeated experience, a pure and unmixed pleasure to have a goodly volume lying before you, and to know that you may open it if you please, and need not open it unless you please. It is a resource against *ennui*, if *ennui* should come upon you." Dr. Folliott also expresses Peacock's distaste for the novels of Sir Walter Scott. Comparing "the literature of pantomime" and "the pantomime of literature," he says, "There is the same variety of character, the same diversity of story, the same copiousness of incident, the same research into costume, the same display of heraldry, falconry, ministrelsy, scenery, monkery, witchery, devilry, robbery, poachery, piracy, fishery, gipsy-astrology, demonology, architecture, for-

tification, castrametation, navigation: the same running base of love and battle. The main difference is,
that the one set of amusing fictions is told in music
and action; the other in all the worst dialects of the
English language."

Peacock's last novel, *Gryll Grange*, was published in
1860 when the author was seventy-five, and nineteen
years after the appearance of *Crochet Castle*. Richard
Garnett hinted that it shows some of "the infirmities
of senescence," but his grandson, David, finds it "the
most charming of the novels." George Saintsbury has
written of it most judiciously. He calls it "the last and
mellowest fruit from Peacock's tree." It shows neither
"the grumbling of old age" nor "the marks of failing
powers." There is "an advance in mildness and mellowness" and a "comparative absence of the sharper
and cruder strokes of the earlier work. . . . The wit is
as bright as ever, though less hard." The novel shows
that he still possessed "the satiric power but the improved and remarkable style, and the faculty, if not of
constructing plot yet of creating and presenting character." The satire, as Carl Van Doren pointed out, "is
directed at the pretensions of science, at newspapers,
at innovations in the methods of serving dinner, at
reforming zeal, at 'bestowing the honours of knight-
hood, which is a purely Christian institution, on Jews
and Paynim,' at the whole American continent, all its
people, acts, and customs, at post-prandial orators, at
the scholarship of poets, at spirit-rapping . . . , and
at competitive examinations." But this account gives
all too solemn an impression of this gay and sunny
book.

The novel is composed of the elements common to
Peacock's other conversational novels, but contains
the most elaborate of the planned entertainments, in
this case, "Aristophanes in London," in which most of
the guests are in one or another way involved. The
comedy satirizes most of what Peacock felt were the
evils and follies of the time, including the vogue for

table-tipping. It need hardly be said that reason finally puts these absurdities to flight. The novel also gives us Mr. Mac Borrowdale, Peacock's most genial picture of a Scot, and Peacock puts in his mouth his disapprobation of some of the unfortunate results of widening the suffrage. "Burning houses, throwing dead cats and cabbage-stumps into carriages, and other varieties of the same system of didactics demonstrated the fitness of those who practised them to have representatives in Parliament. So they got their representatives, and many think Parliament would have been better without them." Peacock also invests the figure of the amorous Harry Hedgerow with kindly and touching humor. He is perhaps the best of Peacock's characters from rural life.

The lovers are Morgana Gryll, the Squire's daughter, Miss Niphet, Lord Curryfin, and Mr. Falconer. The charming girls give evidence of Peacock's knowledge of the female character, though they do not have quite the individuality of the heroines of *Nightmare Abbey* and *Crochet Castle*. Lord Curryfin is the first of Peacock's noblemen to be treated sympathetically. At the beginning, he seems likely to be another monomaniacal oddity. "When lecturing became a mania, he had taken to lecturing; and looking about for an unoccupied subject, he had lighted on the natural history of fish, in which he soon became sufficiently proficient to amuse the ladies, and astonish the fishermen in any seaside place of fashionable resort." He is also enthusiastic about universal education, a distaste for which was one of Peacock's own crochets. "He had been caught by the science of pantopragmatics, and firmly believed for a time that a scientific organization for teaching everybody everything would cure all the evils of society." But, as he becomes involved in the plot, he becomes less an oddity, and more an acceptable human being. At first, he is taken with the charms of Miss Gryll and she gives evidence of favoring him. But presently he finds himself more interested in Miss

Niphet, whose coquetry reminds one of Marionetta in *Nightmare Abbey*, and Miss Gryll, although she has encouraged Lord Curryfin, is attracted by the coy reluctance of Mr. Falconer. In the end, of course, these complications are surmounted, and each member of each pair finds himself engaged to the partner of his choice.

Of this quartet, Mr. Falconer is indubitably the most interesting. He resembles Scythrop Glowry of *Nightmare Abbey* and Sylvan Forester of *Melincourt* in his renunciation of the world and his cultivation of a polite degree of melancholy. But he is less self-consciously virtuous than Forester and less of a prig. We encounter him in a situation that, as Saintsbury rightly suggests, is Gilbertian. He lives in an isolated tower and is waited on by seven virtuous sisters whom he has trained to render appropriate music for his delectation. He himself is a devotee of St. Catherine. "He had always placed the *summum bonum* of life in tranquillity and not in excitement." But now he finds himself attracted by the charms of Miss Gryll and jealous of her apparent preference for Lord Curryfin. "He felt that his path was now crossed by a disturbing force, and determined to use his utmost exertions to avoid exposing himself again to its influence. . . . I have aimed at living, like an ancient Epicurean. I had thought myself armed with triple brass against the folds of a three-formed Chimaera. What with classical studies, and rural walks, and a domestic society peculiarly my own, I led what I considered the perfection of life." To the happily married Dr. Opimian, he says, "It must be a dreadful calamity to be in love. . . . To me it would be the worst of all misfortunes." But, encouraged by the matchmaking Doctor, he finds himself acknowledging his love for Miss Gryll but feels that he cannot abandon his seven virginal attendants. In the solution of this problem, Dr. Opimian again plays the marriage agent. He has listened to the woes of Harry Hedgerow, who has received little or no encouragement from one of Falconer's handmaidens. Dr. Opimian tells Harry of the impediment to his union with his beloved, and Harry resourcefully produces six other rustics for the sisters of his sweetheart. Could any denouement more closely resemble that of a Gilbert and Sullivan opera!

But the triumph of *Gryll Grange* is the clergyman, Dr. Opimian, who in my opinion is an even finer characterization than the much admired Dr. Folliott of *Crochet Castle*. Dr. Opimian's tastes and views coincide almost exactly with Peacock's. Dr. Opimian expresses a number of Peacock's most persistent antipathies in a vigorous and amusingly learned conversational style. He describes the "the epitome of a newspaper" as consisting of "specimens of all the deadly sins, and infinite varieties of violence and fraud," of "bear-garden meetings of mismanaged companies, in which directors and shareholders abuse each other in choice terms," of "bursting of bank bubbles," of "societies of all sorts, for teaching everybody everything, meddling with everybody's business and mending everybody's morals," and of "mountebank advertisements, promising the beauty of Helen in a bottle of cosmetics, and the age of Old Parr in a box of pills." He disapproves of the telegraph because it spreads bad news quickly. He does not regard competitive examinations as a reliable means of discovering genuine ability. Of Americans, he says, "I have no wish to expedite communication with Americans. If we could apply the power of electrical repulsion to preserve me from hearing any more of them, I should think that we had for once derived a benefit from science. . . . On the whole, our intercourse with America has been little else than an interchange of vices and diseases." He waxes prophetic when he says, "The time will come when by mere force of numbers the black race will predominate and exterminate the white," or again when he says, "I almost think that it is the ultimate destiny of science to destroy the human race."

More freely than in any of the earlier novels, Peacock used his epigraphs to suggest the topic of a particular   chapter or to express his own view of life. Sometimes they concern love; frequently they speak of the pleasures of wine; most pointedly they express his fundamental Epicureanism. For his first chapter, he has chosen a sentence from his favorite Petronius. "Always and everywhere I have so lived, that I might consume the passing light, as if it were not to return." Later, he cites Philataerus:

> *I pray you, what can mortal man do better,*
> *Than live his daily life as pleasantly*
> *As daily means allow him? Life's frail tenure*
> *Warns not to trust tomorrow.*

or from Persius:

> *Indulge thy Genius, while the hour's thine own:*
> *Even while we speak, some part of it has flown.*
> *Snatch the swift-passing good: 'twill end ere long*
> *In dust and shadow, and an old wife's song.*

In the "Letter to Maria Gisborne," Shelley expressed his view of the future of Peacock's reputation.

> *. . . his fine wit*
> *Makes such a wound, the knife is lost in it;*
> *A strain too learnèd for a shallow age,*
> *Too wise for shallow bigots: let his page,*
> *Which charms the chosen spirits of the time,*
> *Fold itself up for the serener clime*
> *Of years to come, and find its recompense*
> *In that just expectation.*

When, in 1837, Peacock's first four novels were to be reprinted as Volume LVII of Bentley's "Standard Novels," he was persuaded to write a preface, since old friends had assured him that "to publish a book without a preface is like entering a drawing-room without making a bow." He admitted that some of the follies he had attacked in these novels no longer existed, but that there were still numerous manifestations of humanity's capacity for error. "Literary violaters of the confidences of private life still gain a disreputable livelihood and an unenviable notoriety. Match makers from interest and the disappointed in love and friendship, are varieties of which specimens are extant. The great principle of the Right of Might is as flourishing as in the days of Maid Marion: the array of false pretensions, moral, political, and literary, is as imposing as ever." Most modern readers would agree that the errors to which mankind was susceptible in 1837 are as current today as they were over a century ago, and the frequent republication of Peacock's novels suggests that in every generation of readers there will be a few eccentrics who will savor with delight Peacock's idiosyncratic fictions.

ROBERT SMITH SURTEES

Charles Alva Hoyt

ROBERT SMITH SURTEES is a neglected author to whom
our century might very well look both for entertainment and instruction. To be sure Surtees (1803–64) is
a minor novelist, in the most accepted sense of the
term: he is a specialist, a sporting writer, and the best
in our language. Unfortunately that is where many of
the anthologies leave him, on the tips of the tongues
of doctoral candidates, from which bad eminence he
is let fall, from time to time, into discussion.

Even these excursions must be rare for him today;
young scholars on the prowl want material of greater
"significance." And yet they would do well to remember Louis Kronenberger's description of Don Juan's
adventures in England: "a stiff ride with the hounds
after hypocrites and snobs; a long day on the moors
bagging philistines and pharisees; a large coaching
party clattering at the heels of politics." [1] As Kronenberger suggests, sport to the British is not idle amusement, but their way of life. A British sporting writer
then, if he is a good one, will have a great deal to say
about his time. Surtees was the best, and his opinions
of nineteenth-century British society are both wise
and diverting: vigorous, unsparing, almost always
highly critical. His irony is intense, his indignation
warm, although he frequently melts into long passages
of sheer fun, and nonsense, that sole delight among
Victorian virtues. For these and other reasons he re-

mains easy to read; I find him one of the most congenial of the nineteenth-century novelists.

His deficiencies are almost entirely in technique, and even there confined to few, if important, considerations. His style is rich, anecdotal, Dickensian. In his pervasive irony, however, he more resembles Thackeray, with whom he corresponded and sometimes consulted about his books. But even more than Thackeray he is ever the satirist, a fact which our textbooks too often ignore, although it was understood perfectly in his day. A member of Parliament writes to him as follows, *circa* 1858, "You are all-powerful in exposing pretence, shams, and ostentation, etc., etc., and in gathering up small traits or evidences to crush the culprits. . . . There is only one defect which I should like to hint at. Why not make your satire effective by restraint? Do give us a *good* character, man or woman; honest, truthful, domestic, trying to do what duty requires to God and man, and happy accordingly."[2]

Surtees was then a severe monitor of the morals of his age. How did he come to be so? At this point it is profitable to inquire into his background. When we learn that he was a younger son of a famous old county family, with a superb heritage but very few prospects, we come close to understanding the tone of his novels. He did not attend Oxford or Cambridge, but was articled to one Robert Anthony Purvis, "a leading solicitor of Newcastle." He was later further articled to another man, but at no time can he be said to have taken much interest in his law career. Rather he was assiduous in attending meetings of foxhounds, for which he became so well-known that we find him, in 1830, a regular contributor to the old *Sporting Magazine*.[3] Surtees was none of your gentleman contributors. In fact, it was a disagreement about money which led to his leaving the paper to found his own. He offered first to buy into the company; when denied, he went into partnership with the celebrated print dealer and publisher, Rudolph Ackermann. Between them they set up the *New Sporting Magazine*, with Surtees as editor; and drawing off all of the old *Sporting's* best writers, soon put their rival into eclipse.

At this period Surtees was a regular touring sports-writer. True, he was technically a gentleman, and it was an important technicality, since it insured him a welcome in the proper circles, but as we have seen he was a realist about his position. He showed both resourcefulness and resolution in his financial affairs, and he took part in the journalistic combats of the time with gusto. As his biographer observes, "Surtees was a dangerous foe to attack. He demolished the charges brought against him with the pointed satire of which he was a master." [4]

Furthermore, sporting literature in the nineteenth century, while entirely fit for male consumption, was not proper fare for all occasions, as Surtees himself was aware. Speaking of some sporting pieces projected for the *Quarterly*, that organ of orthodoxy founded by Sir Walter Scott and John Murray, he says: "Mr. Lockhart, who was a capital editor, conceived that many of his subscribers might like to read a well-written article or two on our national sports and pastimes who yet would not like to see a 'Sporting Magazine' lying on their table" [5] Lockhart had come a long way from the days when, as "The Scorpion" of Blackwood's, he had stung Keats to the heart.

Surtees felt all the inconveniences of his semire-spectability, if we may judge from his books. At the same time it gave him certain priceless advantages as a novelist. He was neither out nor in, but something of an outside insider, a privileged commentator with status roughly comparable (if one can bear the thought) to that of today's society columnist, who knows everyone and goes everywhere, yet is neither apart from, nor a part of, all that he describes.

He was not long to remain in limbo. The very year that launched him as an editor brought the death of his elder brother, and he became heir to the family estates. He continued his editorship for five more years but dropped the law at once. "After the event of 1831," as Cuming delicately puts it, "there was no reason why he should continue in a profession that was uncongenial to him." [6] It is the more pleasant, and instructive, then, to observe that he kept to his editor's desk until 1836.

Early in 1838 his father died, and Surtees succeeded to his inheritance, taking up residence at his seat, Hamsterley Hall, near Newcastle. He had been toying with politics, but nothing much came of it, and so he settled to the life of a squire and the problems of agricultural reform—all of which topics were presently to make their appearance in the novels, now gathering shape in his mind with the advent of leisure time.

Surtees' principal publications are as follows: his famous "Jorrocks" sketches were collected in 1838 as *Jorrocks's Jaunts and Jollities*. *Handley Cross*, a full length portrait of Jorrocks, and Surtees' most celebrated work, came out in octavo in 1843. Like Rogers' *Italy*, it languished until illustrations were provided for it, when it blossomed out into parts (March, 1853–October, 1854). *Hillingdon Hall*, a Jorrocks sequel, followed in 1845, again without illustrations (they appeared for the first time in the 1888 edition). *Hawbuck Grange*, probably his weakest book, came out in 1847, after having originally been published in *Bell's Life*, 1846–47; the admirable *Mr. Sponge's Sporting Tour*, in 1853, after a run in parts. *Ask Mamma* appeared in octavo in 1858, *Plain or Ringlets* in 1860, and *Mr. Facey Romford's Hounds* posthumously in 1865. All these last had appeared first in parts; like the others, they were brought out anonymously, as was Surtees' scholarly but whimsical *Analysis of the Hunting Field* in 1846. The only book to which he ever signed his name was his first, the slender and now extremely rare *Horseman's Manual*, 1831.[7]

All of these works were illustrated, whether sooner or later, by first-rate artists, usually John Leech and sometimes "Phiz" (Hablot K. Browne) and Henry Alken. These associations are important ones; we tend to forget that the path between writer and illustrator in the nineteenth century was likely to be a two-way street. The famous *Tours* of Dr. Syntax, set down by Combe in jigging measures, were conceived as decorations for the pictures of Samuel Rowlandson; and by the same token the text of Thomas Bewick's *Quadrupeds* exists only as setting for Bewick's animal drawings and ingenious tail-pieces. It was the artist's name only which appeared. Even Dickens got his first important assignment as a text-provider for a series of sketches of Cockney sportsmen by Robert Seymour. The writer proved too much for the artist in this case, however, and insisted that the pictures serve the text and not vice-versa. Seymour's untimely death (he was a suicide) removed the last difficulty and *The Pickwick Papers* became, not an artistic, but a literary masterpiece.

Thackeray was also a well-known illustrator; in some of his earlier work it is difficult to tell which side of his genius provides the impetus. It was to him that Surtees originally applied for illustrations for his own novels. The note of refusal was polite, and more important, helpful, for it introduced Surtees to Leech, with whom he afterwards carried on what must be thought of, in a sense, as a collaboration, and a highly successful one. The artist suggested numerous items for the books and surely did much to help sell them. It was his name after all, that appeared on the title page. The two men worked together in perfect sympathy: when one says "Jorrocks," one thinks almost immediately of Leech's marvellous drawings, the stout indomitable figure in his pink coat, thundering at the head of the banquet table, or cursing his horse, Artaxerxes, over a hedge.

"You would find my pictures anything but comical," Thackeray had written, begging off, "and I have not the slightest idea how to draw a horse, a dog, or a sporting scene of any sort." [8] There is the heart of the matter, of course—the special requirements of the literature of Sport. They are as binding upon the novelist as upon the illustrator. Surtees' chosen subject matter is at once a bane and a blessing: it requires a special knowledge and a special style, both of which I now propose to take up.

All of Surtees' novels are focussed squarely upon hunting, although some spend longer than others in coming to the subject, and some wander freely from it. I think we may set it down as an axiom that the more the books have to do with hunting, the better they are. It is not because Surtees is knowledgeable only upon the one subject, but, apparently, that he is happiest there. The young man who left the law to follow the hounds all over England, who resisted respectability for five years from his editor's desk, had but one great love in life. " 'Untin is the foremost passion of my 'eart! compared with it all others are flat and unprofitable (cheers and laughter). It's not never of no manner of use 'umbuggin the matter, but there's no sport fit to hold the candle to fox-'untin'." Thus his alter ego, Jorrocks (*Handley Cross*, p. 235), the one major character in his fiction to whom we may say that he gave his wholehearted approval. Jorrocks, too, the sporting Cockney, was always something of an outsider—but we shall reserve him for the last.

Surtees was one of the keenest foxhunters of a generation of eager sportsmen. In the course of his profession as touring writer he made himself familiar with every hunting country in England, just as a seasoned sportswriter today knows every city in the league. But much more than baseball is the American game, foxhunting was the sport of the ruling class in nineteenth-century England. It was in fact participated in by members of all classes, from the notorious hunting tailors and grocers of Surrey (Jorrocks was one such),

representative of the middle class on the way up, to
the sturdy farmers over whose fields the sport was
pursued, and the common laborers themselves who
frequently followed the hounds on foot. The fox-
hunter, as appears over and over again in the novels,
was welcome everywhere. A pink coat would procure a
man entry into the most select society, or get him a
drink at the lowest hovel. As Seymour delighted to
show, the prentices and clerks of the City of London
poured out of town every Sunday, in a motley display
of costumes and weaponry, to engage in fearful struggles with polecats and pushcarts, cucumber frames
and cows.

But just that strength of subject matter has proven
Surtees' downfall in our day, when fox hunting is
known to few and practiced by even fewer. If the
popularity of the sport insured the hunting novelist a
wide audience in the nineteenth century, whatever his
faults, so its decay in the twentieth serves to keep him
in obscurity in spite of his virtues.

So much for the special knowledge required; there
is a similar difficulty involved with the special style.
All arts have their mysteries, one of which is a sacred
language. The sacred language attached to a lost art is
rough going, and that is Surtees' problem in a nut-
shell. But here too is a positive side: there is such a
thing as the fertile cliché. It exists on the outward
circumference of style, where it is not only unavoid-
able but useful, comfortable, and reassuring. Anyone
who enjoys baseball, or Baroque music, or literary
criticism, must know what I mean. If Surtees suffers
from the restrictions of his special language, he also
enjoys the stability, security, and comfort it imparts to
his style. Consider the following passage, chosen practically at random, and from one of the lesser works:

> Mr. Boggledike was again to be seen standing erect in
> his stirrups, yoiking and coaxing his hounds into Crash-
> ington Gorse. There was Dicky, cap-in-hand, in the

centre ride, exhorting the young hounds to dive into the strong sea of gorse. "Y-o-o-icks! wind him! y-o-o-icks! pash him up!" cheered the veteran, now turning his horse across to enforce the request. There was his lordship at the high corner as usual, ensconced among the clump of weatherbeaten blackthorns—thorns that had neither advanced nor receded a single inch since he first knew them,—his eagle eye fixed on the narrow fern and coarse grass-covered dell down which Reynard generally stole. There was Harry Swan at one corner to head the fox back from the beans, and Tom Speed at the other to welcome him away over the corn-garnered open. And now the whimper of old sure-finding Harbinger, backed by the sharp "yap" of the terrier, proclaims that our friend is at home, and presently a perfect hurricane of melody bursts from the agitated gorse,—every hound is in the paroxysm of excitement, and there are five-and-twenty couple of them, fifty musicians in the whole! "*Tally-ho!* there he goes across the ride!"

"*Cub!*" cries his lordship.

"*Cub!*" responded Dicky.

"*Crack!*" sounds the whip.—(*Ask Mamma,* pp. 48–49)

And so "the whole infuriated phalanx dashed across the ride," and off they go, out of our sight. The passage does not present any particularly interesting or unusual character, like Soapey Sponge or Jorrocks' huntsman, James Pigg. It varies in no important particulars from a thousand others in the sporting literature of the time: the technical terms, the affectionate Victorian circumlocutions—"our friend is at home"—"the veteran"—and the cast, as closely prescribed as in an Oriental drama: the Squire, the field, huntsmen, rustics, horses, hounds, fox.

The technical terms, unlike those of some crafts, are easy to master, and the circumlocutions and other assorted gewgaws of Victorian expression may as well seem quaint and charming to us as offensive, now that we have condemned them so utterly in our own fiction. As for the classic situation and its cast, I welcome them with the same affection that I might show a favorite piece of Baroque woodwind music. Indeed the whole passage seems to me like nothing as much as the imperative opening blast of a quartet by K. P. E. Bach, pregnant with good things to come, things which lose none of their value because one knows what they are to be.

Special pleas to one side, it becomes necessary to attempt some evaluation of Surtees' accomplishment as novelist. And immediately it must be said that he is deficient in one vitally important area—design. His weakness is the more noticeable, appearing as it does against the great strengths of many of his contemporaries, who surely have never been surpassed as systematic observers of human life. With Surtees, however, it is otherwise: he grasps situations with incisive wit and draws individuals brilliantly; but in the managing of large movements or character development he is rarely successful. *Ask Mamma*, for example, is very unsure in direction from the start, and *Hawbuck Grange* is little better than a pastiche of anecdotal fragments. In many of his better books, too, he is forced to take hold of the plot from time to time and wrench it into the direction in which he wishes it to go. The death of Jack Spraggon at the end of *Mr. Sponge's Sporting Tour* serves no purpose whatever that I can see, save to get him out of the way; similarly the sudden good fortune that descends upon the hero of *Plain or Ringlets* seems nothing more than a last desperate measure to punish the mercenary women who have been misusing him.

Of these weaknesses Surtees himself was aware. In the preface to *Handley Cross* he says, "The reader will have the kindness to bear in mind, that the work merely professes to be a tale, and does not aspire to the dignity of a novel." There is sarcasm there, perhaps, but self-knowledge as well. Before *Ask Mamma*, he writes, "It may be a recommendation to the lover of light literature to be told, that the following story does not involve the complication of a plot." Certainly Surtees tended to counteract his weakness by slipping into the picaresque, which he does with great success in *Mr. Sponge's Sporting Tour.* "Soapey" Sponge, a delightful fraud and confidence man, but a keen sportsman, methodically works his way through one unsuspecting family after another on his tour, playing upon his well-to-do hosts' and hostesses' crassness and greed. Similarly, the movements of the hunt give a picaresque flavor to *Handley Cross* as well as to *Mr. Romford's Hounds,* whose hero, "Facey" Romford, is like Sponge a confidence man who fattens on the cupidity of his victims.

Subtlety, then, and sophisticated development, of plot, theme, or character, is not to be found here. But what a great deal else is! First of all, the wit and humor, the continuous crackle of exploded pretensions and hypocrisies. Surtees has the columnist's feeling for situation. His perception may lack depth or scope, but the reader may supply these for himself if the author has but caught the situation accurately. At times Surtees apprehends it perfectly.

Here is Soapey Sponge in a dilemma, in chapter forty-four. He is gobbling down his breakfast to be off to the meet, but his hostess, Mrs. Jogglebury Crowdey, who imagines him to be rich, is determined that he shall hear Gustavus James, age two, recite. She hopes to inveigle Soapey into becoming the baby's godfather.

> The child, who had been wound up like a musical snuffbox, then went off as follows: —
>
>> *"Bah, bah, black sheep, have 'ou any 'ool?*
>> *Ess, marry, have I, three bags full;*
>> *Un for ye master, un for ye dame,*
>> *Un for ye 'ittle boy 'ot 'uns about ye 'ane."*
>
> But, unfortunately, Mr. Sponge was busy with his breakfast, and the prodigy wasted his sweetness on the desert air. . . .
>
> "A little more (puff) tea, my (wheeze) dear," said

Jogglebury, thrusting his great cup up the table.

"*Hush!* Jog, *hush!*" exclaimed Mrs. Crowdey, holding up her forefinger, and looking significantly first at him, and then at the urchin.

"Now, 'Obin and Ichard,' my darling," continued she, addressing herself coaxingly to Gustavus James.

"No, *not* 'Obin and Ichard,' " replied the child.

The scene works to its climax over the impending recital of "Obin and Ichard," which Gustavus James manages to delay until the men are at the door.

"Very beautiful!" exclaimed Mr. Sponge; "very beautiful! One of Moore's, isn't it? Thank you, my little dear, thank you," added he, chucking him under the chin, and putting on his hat to be off.

"O, but stop, Mr. Sponge!" exclaimed Mrs. Jogglebury, "You haven't heard it all—there's more yet."

They do not make the meet.

Perhaps one of the most painful scenes in the English novel is described in Chapters Thirty-four and Thirty-five of *Hillingdon Hall*. By this point in the book, which is perhaps Surtees' best planned, Mrs. Flather, a clergyman's widow and a relentless social climber, has succeeded in persuading herself that the Duke and Duchess of Donkeyton will welcome the marriage of her daughter, Emma, to their only son, the Marquis of Bray. Upon the basis of a total misunderstanding with the Duke, who has been clearly revealed to the reader as a monument of aristocratic arrogance, she has made her way to the castle and into the presence of the Duchess, who is somewhat confused.

"Your Grace," again attempted Mrs. Flather, with the desperate energy of a person bent upon a subject, "I am sure you, as a mother, will excuse the — —" . . ."I am sure I need not say," continued she, "how deeply I appreciate the honour conferred on my poor girl."

Her Grace smiled and bowed courteously, thinking it merely had reference to the party she had had them to, and said, "pray don't mention it."

This rather put Mrs. Flather out, and her Grace was just going to draw her attention to the flower-stand beaming radiant before the window—another safety valve for country stupidity—when Mrs. Flather again went on.

Surtees lets the scene dawdle on from one contretemps to the next until Mrs. Flather's frail bark runs up against the horrid rock of financial settlements.

"*Settlements!*" exclaimed the Duchess, staring with astonishment.

"Oh, just as your Grace pleases," replied Mrs. Flather most submissively; "of course we don't insist upon anything of the sort."

"I fear we misunderstand each other," said the Duchess, reconsidering all that had passed. "It surely isn't Jeems you're thinking about? *It can't* be Jeems!" added she, as the ancestry of twenty generations flashed upon her mind. Mrs. Flather felt as if she would drop through the floor before the Duchess's withering glance.

In the kindest possible way her Grace attempts to disabuse Mrs. Flather. "I must tell you as a friend, that it would be the death of the Duke to mention such a thing to him." Nevertheless the wretched woman persists—"But his Grace encouraged it!"—and so, while the reader sits helplessly by, she is allowed to put her case to Donkeyton himself.

She is not able to do so, however, until after an interminable luncheon. Then, "an old woman being as bad to turn as a sheep," she is ushered into the Ducal presence.

the deep snore he every now and then emitted, clearly proclaimed that his Grace slept.

He was quite comfortable. His mouth was wide open, his legs were stretched out before him, his eye-glasses hung on his unbuttoned buff-waistcoat as they had fallen from his nose. . . . A large "blue-bottle" fly buzzed and bumped and noised about the room, now exploring the Duke's bald head, now settling on his nose, now apparently determining to enter his noble

mouth. The impudence of a blue-bottle passes all comprehension.

Having awakened her man, Mrs. Flather comes
straight to her tale, for once, but the scene is not yet
over. The Duke not supposing that marriage can enter
the question, spends most of his part of the conversation clucking about heedless youth. Finally he remarks that he doesn't see that any harm has been
done. " 'None if your Grace encourages the match,'
observed Mrs. Flather boldly. *'Encourage the
match!'* " The Duchess fortunately returns at this
point.

> "Susan, my dear!" exclaimed he, in a towering pas-
> sion, "Mrs. Flather has done us the honour of coming
> here to claim our son in marriage for her daughter."
> "Indeed!" replied the Duchess mildly, well knowing
> there was no occasion for them both to set on her at
> once.
> "Compliment! great compliment! monstrous great
> compliment! isn't it?" asked the Duke, white as his
> whiskers.
> "Perhaps if you are satisfied *now*," observed the
> Duchess with an emphasis, to Mrs. Flather, "you had
> better retire; his Grace is not very well to-day," added
> she, in an undertone, "and does not like to be dis-
> turbed."
> Mrs. Flather took the hint.

To complete her humiliation, she has to suffer afterwards the chaff of Jorrocks, to whom she has impru-
dently let slip some hint of the business. " 'Let the
halmond paste be a hinch thick at least [on the wed-
ding cake]. Never mind about Cupids or cherrybins,
or none o' them gentry; *for me*, at least,' added he."

These two passages were chosen to demonstrate
Surtees' powers of observation and technique, but
they also serve as indications of his social criticism.
Most of his humor is the result of his perception of
the inequalities and absurdities of British society. It
may be mild, as in the case of the incident of Gus-

tavus James, but it is insistent. The Jogglebury Crow-
deys would have thrown Sponge out of the house if
they had known him to be penniless—and as a matter
of fact they eventually do. But by that time Soapey
has got everything he wanted out of them.

These inquiries gentle and sarcastic into British life
play a critical role in Surtees' characterization, which
is made up of a choice lot of rogues and fools—as the
M.P. remarked, there is hardly a decent person among
them. They are all either wolves or sheep. There are,
however, some exceptions; and exceptions do not
make rules; they break them. The half-dozen lovable
characters in Surtees' fiction, with all their faults,
atone for whole legions of his mutton-headed squires,
thieving servants, and rotten society women.

One of the most endearing characteristics of Surtees
is that he loves a good rascal. Both Soapey Sponge and
Facey Romford are crooks; they make a handsome
living cheating respectable people. Yet he gives them
nerve and stamina and flair—hunters' virtues. If they
live on other people's money, they live with style.
They are no Robin Hoods, however. Facey is in fact a
considerable skinflint, as far as his own limited funds
are concerned, and he is callous, insensitive, crude and
ignorant to boot. Soapey is selfish, irresponsible, tact-
less and impertinent. Yet they can ride, and will ride,
and nothing can stop them. Like their creator, they
esteem nothing so much as fox hunting.

These men are at the head of Surtees' list of rogues.
He has many, many more. A good Surtees novel begins with a hunt and a ball, a banquet and a by-day,
and ends with a marriage, an election, or a bank-
ruptcy. In between we have seen hunt society in action: the men trying to sell each other horses; the
women, their daughters. This society, as I have suggested, is conceived of by Surtees and his time as
including practically everybody. There are rich families looking for titles, titled families looking for riches;
poor boys trying to pass themselves off as Earls, and

poor girls posing as heiresses. The rich are too often proud, and the poor either envious or craven.

All these dinner parties and dances are in reality fine dressing for a primitive and rather ugly business: buying and selling innocent flesh, and it is a clear case of *caveat emptor*. The buyer is, in fact, almost always cheated, Surtees seems to say, because he has tried to purchase with money that which he should have sought out with an honest heart. If this statement makes Surtees a moralist, so be it. There is no other explanation for his constant attack on Victorian morality.

For it is the "respectable people" who lose, time and again, in every novel. Who wins? Jorrocks, but he is a presumptuous cockney and an unashamed bourgeois, a tea merchant held in disdain by the wealthy Mrs. Barnington and her set. Soapey Sponge and Facey Romford escape to Australia with whole skins and a bit of money after having led the gentry a pretty dance. But old Goldspink, the prosperous banker of *Ask Mamma*, is ruined in business in spite of all his cleverness.

These greedy respectable people are the legitimate prey of frauds, whether professionals like Soapey and Facey, or amateurs like "Fine Billy" Pringle, a harmless simpleton, the hero of *Ask Mamma*, who has somehow acquired a reputation as "the richest commoner in England." Of course he has next to nothing, but he lives very well at the expense of all the greedy mammas who would rather be humbugged ten times over than lose a good prospect to a rival.

Then there are the exotic frauds, like Prince Pirouetteza, the son of a Florentine dancing master, who turns up in *Plain or Ringlets* as house guest of the great Duke of Tergiversation, or Sir Moses Mainchance of *Ask Mamma*, the stock villainous Jew of fiction, wealthy and crass. Sir Moses, however, with the advent of his baronetcy, has embraced the principles of the Church of England.

These outlandish characters are rare; much better can be found right at home. There is Robert Foozle of *Sponge's Sporting Tour*, a gentleman of good family.

> Young lady: "Were your sisters out to-day?"
> Foozle: "Yes, my sisters were out to-day."
> Young lady: "Are your sisters going to the Christmas ball?"
> Foozle: "Yes, my sisters are going to the Christmas ball."
>
> . . . .
> Sponge: "Are you fond of hunting?"
> Foozle: 'Yes, I'm fond of hunting."
> Jawleyford: "But you *don't* hunt, you know, Robert."
> Foozle: "No, I don't hunt."

"Robert was the hope of the house of Foozle," Surtees says, "and it was fortunate his parents were satisfied with him, for few other people were." "Still, nearly daft as Robert was, he was generally asked where there was anything going on; and more than one young la——but we will not tell about that, as he has nothing to do with our story" (pp. 117–19). The young girls come in for severe criticism from time to time, for not only acquiescing in their parents' marriage-settlement game, but taking an active part in it on their own.

Then there are *nouveaux riches* like Willy Watkins of *Mr. Romford's Hounds*, "a good-looking fellow without any brains," who has fallen into money somehow in the never-never land Australia, and returned home with a horror of a wife, the sort "who would push her way if she could." There is a marriageable daughter, Cassandra Cleopatra, descended on her father's side of ne'er-do-wells, and on her mother's of deported felons. The Watkins family carries on a duel for honors with Mr. and Mrs. Hazey of a landed family of dubious character. And there are mountebanks and quack doctors—Sebastian Mello, the fastidious fraud of *Handley Cross*—and common cardsharpers—Johnny O'Dicey of *Plain or Ringlets*—all the jackals and kites who lurk at the edges of society. But we have had enough of them.

Truly good men and women are rare in Surtees, as in life, but worth the search. The parade of his characters in their ceaseless vanity reminds one of Hieronymus Bosch's painting, "The Hay Wain." There all mankind is represented as struggling forward in foolish dispute over an enormous load of straw which is rolling them straight to Hell, while far above all the scuffling and shouting two lovers dally, on top of the world as it were, protected from its nonsense by the purity of their emotion. Just so Surtees exempts from his indictment the honest sportsman, the rare man who forsakes worldliness for love. Such a one is Jovey Jessup; several times referred to in the canon, and fully portrayed in *Plain or Ringlets:* "a thorough sportsman and a hearty hospitable fellow." He keeps two cooks, "an Englishman to cook his beefsteak for breakfast, and a Frenchman to send up the fricandeau, etc., for dinner." When his digestion is threatened because of his unceasing dinners and drinking bouts, he does not become a recluse, but rather takes on a fellow to do his drinking for him, a Mr. Boyston who is thereafter known as Jovey Jessup's Jug.

Delightful as these two are, they are eclipsed by Jorrocks and his famous Scotch huntsman, James Pigg ("dinna call me a Scotchman, and keep thy bit bowdekite quiet—ar'll manish matters").

"Oh, beautiful! beautiful!" exclaimed Mr. Jorrocks, in raptures, as each hound put his nose to the ground. . . . " 'Ow true to the line! best 'ounds in England, by far—never were such a pack!". . .

"Hould hard, ye sackless ould sinner!" now cried Pigg, crossing the main ride at a canter, and nearly knocking Jorrocks off his horse. . . .

. . . .

"*Tally ho!*" now screamed Jorrocks, . . ."Oh, Pigg, wot a wopper he is!" The biggest fox whatever was seen —"if we do but kill him—my vig! I'll eat his tongue for

supper. Have it grilled 'cum grano salis,' with a lee-tle
Cayenne pepper, as Pomponius Hego would say."

"Aye," replied Pigg, grinning with delight, his cap-
peak in the air and the tobacco-juice streaming down
his mouth like a Chinese Mandarin. "Ar'll be the *death
of a shillin*' mysel'!"—(*Handley Cross*, pp. 183–84)

It is love between these two, although the word is
never mentioned. Here is Pigg stone-drunk, not an
unusual situation for him, greeting his master at the
start of a meet: "'a—a—a sink! . . . here's canny ard
sweetbreeks hissel! . . . a—a—a, but ar de like to see
his feulish 'ard feace a grinnin' in onder his cap! . . .
How way, canny man, how way! and give us a wag o'
thy neif' "—(*Handley Cross*, p. 279) A coolness
springs up at this familiarity, but when Pigg sobers up
and rejoins the hunt at the critical moment, all is
forgiven. The other huntsmen prove useless: "Come
on, ye miserable, useless son of a lily-livered besom-
maker," Jorrocks roars at one hesitating at a fearful
leap; "Rot ye, I'll bind ye 'prentice to a salmon
pickler!" Then Pigg appears and the hounds kill their
fox.

"O Pigg, you're a brick! a fire brick!" gasps the heavily perspiring Mr. Jorrocks, throwing himself exhausted
from his horse. . . . "O Pigg, *let us fraternise!*"
Whereupon Jorrocks seized Pigg by the middle, and
hugged him like a Polar bear, to the mutual astonishment of Pigg and the Pack.—(*Handley Cross*, p. 292)

Hunting, hunting, is Jorrocks' life, but not his only
life. Like other great men he plays many parts. Hunting is undoubtedly his preferred role, but Surtees
brings him on so that we see him from every side of
his imposing personality. In the early sketches we
know him as a great merchant of London, an eccentric, already famous as a fox hunting enthusiast.
Handley Cross brings him down to the country and
into country society, as a Master of Fox Hounds—the
apex of his ambition. Finally, in *Hillingdon Hall*, he

buys an estate and establishes himself as a squire—Justice of the Peace and all. The book ends with his winning an election over the Marquis of Bray by two votes and going into Parliament.

It is Dick Whittington all over again. And indeed Jorrocks is precisely of that tradition, a tradition as honorable and old as London itself. He is the heir to those prosperous city merchants of the old drama, the "flat-caps" of Shakespeare's day who held firm to their principles although scorned by sprigs of quality. Dekker's great Simon Eyre of *The Shoemaker's Holiday* is one such, and Marston's Master Touchstone of *Eastward Ho* another. Their liberality, their geniality, their prudence and good sense were at the heart of English prosperity, and the old playwrights knew it. Jorrocks is just such another. He has not an ounce of pretense or sham about him; when snobs patronize him by adding an order for tea to their correspondence about fox hunting, he dutifully fills the order before telling them to go to the devil.

> "Pray, Mr. Jorrocks, who was your mother?" inquired his Grace, after he had bowed and drank off his wine.
>
> "Please your Greece, my mother was a washerwoman."
>
> "A *washerwoman, indeed!*" exclaimed his Grace—"that's very odd—I like washerwomen—nice, clean, wholesome people—I wish my mother had been a washerwoman."
>
> "I vish mine had been a duchess," replied Mr. Jorrocks.—(*Hillingdon Hall*, p. 98)

It seems to me that it is very much to Surtees' credit that he made this man the central figure of his fiction. Surely the fact destroys the objection brought by the M.P., that his satire is unrelenting. Although he has a good deal of fun with Jorrocks, he never patronizes him, no, nor betrays him, either. Whatever Surtees may have lacked as a novelist, it was not what is popularly called *class*.

And thus it is possible to say that he was not entirely disillusioned with his country either, for although he looked unflinchingly at its faults, he believed that in it a man like Jorrocks might still rise from a grocer's apprenticeship to great wealth, popularity in the highest circles, and finally to parliament. The parallels are by no means exact, but Surtees put a great deal of himself into Jorrocks: both were men absolutely devoted. This honest, unpretentious devotion, in both cases, justified and dignified its subject, and incidentally led both men, if we may judge by what Surtees' friends have written of him, away from shallowness and vanity into lives of decency, happiness, and merit.

BENJAMIN DISRAELI

Bernard McCabe

"NOTHING is so easy as to laugh. . . . We remember the amatory eclogue, the old loves and the new loves in which so much passion and recrimination is mixed up between the noble Lord, the Tityrus of the Treasury Bench, and the learned Daphne of Liskeard. . . . When we remember at the same time that with emancipated Ireland and enslaved England, on the one hand a triumphant nation, on the other a groaning people, and notwithstanding the noble Lord, secure on the pedestal of power, may wield on one hand the keys of St. Peter, and. . . ." The shouts that followed drowned the rest, so the *Times* of December 8, 1837, tells us; for this is Disraeli, luxuriantly curled, loaded with gold, splendid in dandiacal bottle green; and addressing the House of Commons for the first time. His maiden speech, as elaborately and inappropriately brilliant as his appearance, was treated by the down-to-earth M.P.'s as absurd, greeted in fact with "hisses, groans, hoots, catcalls, drumming with feet, loud conversation and the imitation of animals."

Brilliance and absurdity. These might seem very useful terms with which to sum up Disraeli the novelist. Initially at least we see in his books only brittle chatter, bizarre politics, blatant heroics, bloated sentiment, a medley of brilliant absurdities, a medley with considerable entertainment value (if of rather recherché appeal) and nothing more.

In his political career, however, though he never perhaps lost a faint tinge of absurdity, Disraeli rapidly became something more than a brilliant entertainer. That first speech of his ended with a suddenly audible and typically accurate Disraelian prophecy: "I sit down now, but the time will come when you will hear me." He was right, of course, and it is not difficult to say why. What made Disraeli more and more audible in the House of Commons was a combination of acute intelligence and a sensitive understanding of what went on there. The same intelligence and sensitivity make it possible for us, often admittedly against considerable odds, to take him seriously as a novelist. In the end what gives Disraeli some claim to stature is a quality that links him, however remotely, to the greatest nineteenth-century novelists: an imaginative and witty awareness, on many levels, of the world in which he was involved.

It is true that this awareness emerges only fragmentarily in the earlier novels, where absurdity abounds. In his first books Disraeli remains largely in a world compounded of personal fantasy and artificial "literariness." Of *Vivian Grey* (1826–27), *Contarini Fleming* (1832), and *Alroy* (1833), Disraeli said, in a private journal: "This trilogy is the secret history of my feelings." He was sounding the deep romantic note, for these first novels are in fact full of what by the late 1820's had become romantic *clichés*. His protagonists, for example, Vivian, Contarini and Alroy, all straining after some ineffable ideal, are all afflicted with the vaguest longings and the darkest melancholy; each is liable to outbursts of unrestrained emotion; each is preoccupied with himself, his destiny and his doom. The décor is determinedly romantic too. Much of the activity in *Vivian Grey* and *Contarini Fleming* takes place before a background of Alps and Apennines, cataracts and chasms; *Alroy* is full of the exotic wonders of the mysterious East. In such surroundings each hero falls in love with an ethereal, almost unattainable beauty.

SOUTHERN ILLINOIS UNIVERSITY PRESS

Carbondale, Illinois

We submit herewith for review

TITLE   "Minor British Novelists"
(Crosscurrents / Modern Critiques
series, edited by Harry T. Moore)

Editor
~~XXXXXXXXX~~   Charles Alva Hoyt. Preface by
Harry T. Moore

PUBLICATION DATE   MAR 1 3 1967

PRICE $4.95

We shall appreciate receiving a copy of any notice that may appear.

Somewhere behind these mannered attitudes there no doubt lies a real impulse towards what Alroy calls "a life full of deep feeling and creative thought," a search for intense experience in the subjective world of emotion and fancy that the great Romantic poets explore. But the trouble with the romanticizing Disraeli is that in the process his emotion quickly becomes commonplace, his fancy cheap.

For the first trilogy brings us immediately face to face with a curious (though typically Victorian) aspect of Disraeli's writing—the persistence in it of a sort of literary dual personality. Disraeli lived in the afterglow of the great Romantics, particularly in the fashionable literary afterglow. The Romantic impact was evidently enormous, and it played upon Disraeli's inherited shrewdness, the eighteenth-century Voltairean matter-of-factness of his father, Isaac D'Israeli, with strangely mixed results. It would be comfortable to be able to treat the two resultant strands in Disraeli's writing with equal respect, to take him seriously on the one hand as a Romantic, a Coleridgean, say, and seriously as a rationalist, or (to complete Mill's useful formula) a Benthamite on the other. But unfortunately more fundamental critical distinctions intervene; too often the choice is not between a fashionable diversity of Disraelian masks but simply between the good and the bad, the fake and the genuine, the original and the secondhand. Nineteenth-century novelists were notoriously uneven; George Eliot, Dickens, Thackeray—many critics have remarked upon the extraordinary gap between their best writing and their worst. Disraeli's is an unusually striking case. Generally, on one side there is the derivative, romantic-sentimental, "literary" novelist, reproducing conventional literary attitudes in the conventional literary language of his day, and on the other the original, ironically intelligent, witty observer and critic of his times.

The two aspects necessitate two styles, clearly distinguishable. This, for instance, is from the first page of *Vivian Grey.*

The child was nearly ten years old and did not know his alphabet, and Mrs. Grey remarked that he was getting ugly. The fate of Vivian Grey was decided. . . . "I'm told, my dear," observed Mrs. Grey, . . . "that Dr. Flummery's would do very well for Vivian. Nothing can exceed the attention which is paid to the pupils. There are sixteen young ladies, all the daughters of clergymen, merely to attend to the morals and the linen: terms moderate: 100 guines per annum, for all under six years, few extras, only for fencing, pure milk, and the guitar." — (I, i, 1) [1]

This is slight enough, of course, and even slightly mannered; but already, with "the morals and the linen," we can catch something of the quality of his best prose: brisk, buoyant, alive. The style is not particularly easy to characterize, but it reproduces the typical quick awareness of the city dweller, the clever Cockney that Disraeli was. It is the language of his journals and the best of his letters; one senses the active mind behind the words, whether he is catching some revealing habit of thought in a snatch of dialogue, or formulating in a few sharp sentences some piece of hypocrisy or folly.

Yet here is Vivian some ten years and some three hundred pages later, when romantic sentiment and elaborate rhetoric have taken control.

And Vivian and his beautiful companion owned the magic of this hour, as all must do, by silence. . . . Oh! who can describe what the o'ercharged spirit feels at this sacred hour, when we almost lose the consciousness of existence, and pure souls seems to struggle to pierce futurity! . . . But now, when he had never felt nature's influence more powerful . . . he started when he remembered that all this was in the presence of a human being! Was it Hesperus that he gazed on, or something else brighter than an Evening star? Even as he thought that his gaze was fixed upon the countenance of nature, he found that his eyes rested on the face of nature's loveliest daughter! — (V, xv, 281)

Disraeli falls into this kind of romantic posturing with great facility. The dichotomy of styles in fact persists throughout his fiction, producing an atmosphere of precariousness that is never quite escapable.

In his first trilogy, what is more, Disraeli seems to lack stamina. Thus the lively brilliance of the original volume of *Vivian Grey*, which scandalized a delighted London public with its cocky Byronic revelations about high life in the city, written in witty imitation of contemporary gossip sheets like *The Age and John Bull*, is quickly dissipated in the succeeding volumes, in which Disraeli takes his hero, an intellectual Don Juan, through a heavily romantic and progressively meaningless Grand Tour. *Contarini Fleming: A Psychological Autobiography* follows a similar pattern. The first volume draws a sensitive portrait of the artist as a young man, written with an intensity that is agreeably relieved by some witty self-awareness. Disraeli had evidently been reading *Wilhelm Meister* (translated by Carlyle in 1826), as well as Byron and Shelley and Alfieri and Voltaire and Schiller and Schlegel and a dozen other romantics whose traces are palpable in *Contarini Fleming*'s text. He was to use the *Bildungsroman* formula again and again in his novels; here he articulates what must have been a real Disraelian as well as a borrowed Goethean dilemma, the conflicting drives toward action in a world of politics, and contemplation in the world of art ("Am I then a poet after all?"). Yet *Contarini Fleming*, which in its early chapters does appear to spring from what Contarini identifies as "my real experience of feeling, my own intelligence, my own observations of incident," collapses when interminable Eastern travels once more begin, and literary attitude-striking takes over. *The Wondrous Tale of Alroy*, Disraeli's historical novel about a "gorgeous incident" in medieval Jewish history, does not really lack stamina, for the author maintains the novel's perfervid absurdity from first to last. "This brilliant fantasy, totally imbued with Vathek" as Beckford admiringly described it, with its experiments in rhymed prose and its snatches of fractured Shakespeare is a real Curiosity of Literature.

Byronism is everywhere in this first trilogy. And if *Vivian Grey* suggests *Don Juan* and *Contarini Fleming, Childe Harold,* the Bryonism in Alroy apes the *Oriental Romances.* (Interestingly, it was Disraeli's father who, in 1797, published *Mejnoun and Leile* as "the first oriental romance in English.") Immediate inspiration for *Alroy* must have come from the contemporary fashion in costume dramas, and Scott's success had made medieval fictions popular. But Disraeli was exploiting a well-worked vein in *Alroy.* English travellers have always found a special fascination in the mysteries and exoticisms of Asia Minor, and never more so than in the age of Eliot, Warburton, and Kinglake. Novels, narrative verse, not to mention *tableaux vivants,* charades, songs at the piano, and other forms of fourth Georgian and early Victorian drawing room art relied heavily on the mysterious and gorgeous East for inspiration. In *Alroy* Disraeli's imagination goes feverishly to work.

> The Princess accepted a spoon made of a single pearl, the long, thin golden handle of which was studded with rubies, and condescended to partake of some saffron soup, of which she was fond. Afterwards she regaled herself with the breast of a cygnet, stuffed with almonds, and stewed with violets and cream. . . . Her attention was then engaged with a dish of those delicate ortolans. . . . Tearing the delicate birds to pieces with her still more delicate fingers, she insisted upon feeding Alroy, who of course yielded to her solicitations.—(IX, II, 188)

The passage illustrates fairly enough a characteristic of Disraeli that was simultaneously laughed at and admired in the nineteenth century: a sort of highly wrought lushness, vulgarity in fact, that runs counter to the astringency of his equally characteristic ironic wit.

One finds this lushness in another form in his "Silver Fork" novels. Silver forks and sentiment inform *The Young Duke* (1831), *Henrietta Temple* (1837) and *Venetia* (1837), novels which may conveniently be grouped as a second trilogy insofar as they are all fashionable novels in the style of the 1830's, when Lady Blessington, Lady Charlotte Bury, and Mrs. Gore were turning out their tales of London society, with minute concern for details of etiquette, dress, and demeanor, at balls, the hunt, Almack's, and Crockford's. Disraeli displays a characteristically ambiguous interest in this world. Although his tongue is clearly in his cheek some of the time, one detects a certain wistful self-indulgence about his lavish accounts of life amongst the very rich in the Young Duke's London ("Your Grace is aware that we may run up some thousands?" "I give you no limit."), or in the flowing demesnes of Henrietta Temple. Disraeli's letters at the time he is writing *Henrietta Temple* and *Venetia* make it clear, though, that they were written to pay some of his debts, and the novels reflect his slight engagement in them. "Is it prudent to bring the domestic history of Childe Harold so strikingly before the public?" asked *The Athenaeum* of *Venetia*, for the novel is an absurdly garbled fictionalizing of some aspects of Byron and Shelley's home life, a sort of bulging expansion of *Julian and Maddalo*. *Henrietta Temple* is an almost equally absurd love story, a high-flown affair whose protagonists are surrounded by that unreal aura of fond benignity common to most popular sentimental fiction. Its language ("methinks I hear the chariot wheels of my bride") has similar overtones, and the lovers' intimate conversation can be excruciating. " 'Those eyes are so brilliant, so very blue, so like the violet! There is nothing like your eyes!' 'Except your own.' " The oddities of Victorian taste are reflected in Tennyson's high regard for this novel;

even more surprising is that Leslie Stephen considered it (with *Contarini Fleming*) to be Disraeli's finest achievement.

Today *The Young Duke* seems the most attractive in this group. Disraeli had evidently intended to write a kind of *Rake's Progress*, and before his invention fades and sentiment replaces irony, or rich rhetoric suppresses the economical wit, there are some splendidly vapid moments that look forward to the club scenes in *Sybil*.

> "My tailor presented me his best compliments, the other morning," said the Duke.
> "The world is growing familiar," said Mr. Annesley.
> "There must be some remedy," said Lord Darrell. . . .
> "It is shocking," said Mr. Annesley, with a forlorn air.—
> (III, VIII, 174)

There is a fine gambling scene in this novel that goes beyond conventional social criticism to reveal the shabby ugliness behind so much fashionable life, but in the end in *The Young Duke* Disraeli's Hogarthian punches are pulled, and there's no real danger of Newgate or Bedlam.

All these early novels are full of autobiographical implications (often uncannily prophetical), and they have been extensively milked by Disraeli's legion of biographers. Vivian, Contarini, and Alroy; the Duke of St. James and Ferdinand Armine in *Henrietta Temple*; and Cadurcis in *Venetia* are all dissatisfied young men in quest of self-fulfilment, beset by an ambition not too sure of its target, conscious that life has something richer to offer than their experience has so far shown. Ferdinand Armine expresses the feeling typically: "A man does not like to give up without a struggle all his chances of romance and rapture." There is often an attractive zest about the way Disraeli tries to involve the reader in these romantic adventurers' quest, but his own uncertainties (so clearly reflected in the vagaries of his prose) reveal a rather thin picture of what romance and rapture really mean to him. The secret histories end in large vague Byronic-Shelleyan gesturings, but in the later novels the golden dream has boiled down to beautiful wives, wealth, and earldoms.

The Silver Fork novels are, generally speaking, thoroughly bad books. Yet before wondering how Disraeli, who as a young man was quite seriously committed to the search for some kind of aesthetic fulfilment (he attempted drama and epic verse in the thirties), could have brought himself to turn out these potboilers, we must remind ourselves of the uncertain status of the novel at this time. Despite the great eighteenth-century pioneers, despite Jane Austen, despite Scott, the associations that the word "novel" aroused amongst most literate people were still mainly frivolous. The novel meant, for many readers, Lady Blessington or Mrs. Gore at best; at worst, something French. Great novels had been written, but the form was not yet the pressing invitation to the serious artist to engage all his abilities in a deeply serious personal commitment.

Yet, as their subtitles suggest, what distinguishes the novels of Disraeli's major trilogy, *Coningsby, or The New Generation* (1844), *Sybil, or The Two Nations* (1845), and to a lesser extent, *Tancred, or The New Crusade* (1847), is a real and sustained seriousness. "Though its form be light and unpretentious," says Disraeli in the last pages of *Sybil*, "the work would yet aspire to suggest to its readers some considerations of a very opposite character." Underlying these novels is a realistic concern with the world in which Disraeli lived, and a real desire to influence opinion about it.

For these are not, like so many of the earlier novels, merely *romans á clef*; they are also *romans á thèse*. The chief interest is less the hero than the society in which he lives; and although the novels bear certain resemblances to the secret histories they now treat of public history. The protagonists are still charming, handsome, greatly gifted young aristocrats who will wander through a troubled self-doubting adolescence toward triumphant marriages with girls of surpassing beauty and surpassing wealth. But Disraeli's intention is new, as he tells us in a General Preface written in 1870: "The derivation and character of political parties; the condition of the people which had been the consequence of them; the duties of the Church as a main remedial agency in our present state." He intended in fact to deal with the condition of England. *Coningsby* paints a picture of post-reform political realities; *Sybil* elaborates it, enlarging the canvas to expose the social realities lying behind the shabby politics; *Tancred* attempts to complete Disraeli's panorama by depicting the spiritual state of the nation.

There is a new maturity here, and lying behind it a great deal of new experience. The first trilogy, after all, had been written largely out of the books in Disraeli's father's library, supplemented with some youthful European travels. His Silver Fork fiction reflects nothing so much as Disraeli's growing acquaintance with fashionable London, in whose more raffish circles he had become a leading figure. But by the time he came to write *Coningsby* Disraeli had been an M.P. for seven years, which gave him insights into political life such as no serious novelist has had before or since. What is more he had now dropped much of his literary affectations (as he had dropped much of his dandyism). In *Coningsby* and *Sybil* Shelley and Schiller are replaced by Reports of Parliamentary Committees, Blue Books and Chartist files. Literary influences are still powerful, but the dominating presence is no longer Byron. Disraeli, like so many other Victorian men-of-letters, had now come under the influence of Carlyle, that ubiquitous stimulator of serious concern.

The major trilogy leaves no doubt, in a series of typically submerged quotations, that the author of

Chartism (1834) and especially *Past and Present* (1843) had made a strong impact. Many of Carlyle's early attitudes, his belief in salvation through an aristocracy, his attachment to individualism and the efficacy of the hero, his own nostalgic glances at a vanished medieval society, echo through *Coningsby, Sybil,* and *Tancred.*

Yet the old Disraeli remains, with all the glitter of fashionable London lavishly described. Romanticism still rears its head, in a new and intriguing form, for Disraeli had now joined forces with Young England. The members of this short-lived but lively political organization, brilliant young noblemen like Lord John Manners and George Smythe (later Lord Strangford), were so Disraelian that if they had not existed he might have invented them. And they in fact became the heroes of his novels. These eager youths combined a quite serious Tory radicalism, which drew its inspiration from a Burke-Coleridge-Southey tradition, with a modish medievalism very much the thing in the late thirties and early forties, the age of the Eglinton Tournament. Disraeli's combination of scathing contempt for Whig opportunism and impatience with old-line Toryism, his slashing indictments of "this perplexed, ill-informed, jaded, shallow generation . . . wearied with the endless ebullitions of their own shallow conceit," his own romantic medievalism, and his imaginatively flamboyant oversimplifications of English political history were evidently irresistible to the young men just down from Cambridge, and they quickly adopted him as their leader.

The personalities of the movement all appear more or less recognizably in the trilogy, and so do its distinctive ideas and attitudes; Young England ambition and enthusiasm, Young England political and social theory, Young England historical and religious preoccupations all inform the books: Young England brilliance is well-represented—but so also is Young England absurdity. And it is a nice critical exercise to determine what is deliberately ironic in Disraeli's treatment of the movement, and what is inadvertently nonsense. For although self-awareness and self-control have greatly developed, the Disraelian dual personality persists in the major trilogy. Young England political romanticism has replaced Byronic literary romanticism, but still Disraeli's commitment is inconstant and uncertain. Thus Young England attitudes simultaneously endorsed and modified by ironic overtones (especially in *Coningsby*) help to dramatize Disraeli's anti-Benthamite attachment to "glory" and "reverence"; but when the pure doctrine obtrudes (as it unmistakably does in *Sybil*) one immediately suspects that these are uneasy romantic novels after all, that serious thinking (and serious feeling) has ceased, that we are back in that theatrical world inhabited by Prince Alroy and the later Contarini Fleming.

Romantic attitudes bring romantic rhetoric; Disraeli's purpler prose reappears in the major trilogy. But *Coningsby* and *Sybil* and at least part of *Tancred* are written much of the time in the hard, clear, witty, "thinking" language, the crisp, economical prose that appears only very intermittently in the earlier novels. Disraeli's voice exposes the inanities and venalities of politicians, in *Coningsby*, for example; it emphasizes the fatal gap between rich and poor in *Sybil* and until it is silenced by a retreat into oriental romanticism, it plays lightly around the inadequacies of the established Church in *Tancred*. The extraordinary parade of caricatures, the Tapers and Tadpoles and Jawster Sharpes is not merely a series of witty comic turns, it is part of the composite commentary on public life that the novels achieve.

It is important, if we are to accept *Sybil* and its companions as novels at all, to see that in them Disraeli is doing much more than presenting a controversial viewpoint. By embodying his theses in the novels he submits his ideas to an imaginative illustration and re-examination of a kind that escapes abstract formulation. For example, Disraeli is much concerned with the changing locus of public power in England, and if we read the trilogy as an interrelated whole we find that in the course of it he has presented the notion of Aristocracy in a dramatized debate which is able to include and reconcile apparently contradictory notions about what aristocracy means. In his *Vindication of the English Constitution* (1835), a volume of political journalism which had already begun to formulate many of the positions he takes up in this trilogy, Disraeli had described the virtues of an aristocracy.

> by ease, by leisure and freedom from anxiety, they are encouraged to the humanizing pursuit of learning and to the liberal pursuit of the arts; an order of men who are born honoured, and taught to respect themselves by the good fame and glory of their ancestors; who from the womb to the grave are taught to loathe and recoil from everything that is mean and sordid, and whose honour is a more precious possession than their parks and palaces. . . .

This admiring attitude is illustrated profusely, exemplified in the person of Coningsby, for example. But the industrialist Millbank advances a totally opposed view in *Coningsby*.

> "I have yet to learn that they are richer than we are, better informed, wiser or more distinguished for public or private virtue. Is it not monstrous that individuals so circumstanced should be invested with the highest conceivable privileges, the privilege of making laws? I say there is nothing in a masquerade more ridiculous!" — (IV, IV, 178–79)

And this attitude, too, the "masquerade," is amply illustrated in *Coningsby*'s Lord Monmouth or *Sybil*'s Lord Marney and Lord Mowbray. Within these extremes various subordinate attitudes appear (notably Disraeli's reiterated view that industrial society produces its own legitimate aristocrats and must recognize them). In the end the novels have animated a complex of meanings.

A similar richness surrounds his attention to representative government. Attacks are frequent: in *Coningsby* it is "the happy device of a ruder age . . . an age of semi-civilisation," in *Tancred* it is a "fatal drollery." Conversely, all three novels exude Disraeli's fascinated absorption in the processes of democratic government. In *Coningsby* particularly we find an intense professional political concern, and an attempt to convey, through his pictures of a corrupt and corrupting society, a firmer indication of what political morality should really mean. *Sybil* adopts what might be called the "Bleak Age" approach to the social condition of England, stressing the miseries that, as every schoolboy knows, the urban and rural poor sustained as a result of the accelerating industrial revolution. Yet *Sybil* was meant to be read in the context of *Coningsby*, and in that novel Disraeli goes out of his way to emphasize the revolution's achievements, insisting upon "the grandeur of Manchester . . . as great a human exploit as Athens." One might add that, if economic historians are right in criticizing the Hammonds for underestimating the advances in living conditions that the revolution brought with it, and if from some long-range viewpoints the local crisis may seem of small account in relation to ultimate economic and social progress (as it did at short range to Macaulay in his well-known review of Southey's *Colloquies*), it is important to realize that in *Sybil* Disraeli was concerned with immediate and dramatic situations, particularly as they presented themselves to the most intelligent and sensitive of contemporary observers. And he found most original ways of presenting these situations.

The live presentation of conflicting values is one of the things a novel can offer that an abstract vindication cannot, and the complex life in the major trilogy provides sufficient answer to the kind of criticism of

Disraeli exemplified in G. K. Chesterton's comment: "His novels are able and interesting considered as everything else except novels." Disraeli himself claimed to be writing primarily" to influence opinion," and the limitations that his diagnostic and didactic preoccupations impose cannot be denied. They exclude a great deal of what the great nineteenth-century novelists made their central concern, the rich psychological realism, the sensitive exploration of individuals in their human relationships. Yet this is not all the story. Disraeli's political novels surely are more than the sum of their isolatable ideas; they do succeed in their own way in dramatizing the complexities (including the absurdities) of human experience, in individual scenes (the climactic scene between Coningsby and his grandfather adds up to much more than the confrontation of two political attitudes—Tadpole and Taper mean more than political corruption), and in their cumulative impact. One might, in this context, place Disraeli beside Thomas Love Peacock, another novelist who devised an idiosyncratic form through which to "seriously apply serious standards" to his age.

Tancred's account of the religious condition of England cannot be taken too seriously, however. Its portraits of fashionable society attempting piety are clever and amusing, but do not come as close to the bone as the wit in *Coningsby* and *Sybil*, perhaps because the positive religious values proposed in contrast are not so convincing as the political and social values of the other novels. *Tancred* masquerades as a kind of theological Bildungsroman, but Disraeli's doctrinal information is so slight that the large and misty generalizations contrast sharply with the expertise in *Coningsby* and *Sybil*. Despite its solemn preambles the novel sometimes seems closer in spirit to the flippancies of *Vivian Grey*.

The book also seems to move back towards *Contarini Fleming* and *Alroy*, as its hero abandons Young England and returns, or escapes to a New Jerusalem, a private Disraelian world of hothouse orientalism, where London's silver forks become golden spoons and clashing scimitars, chibouques, and yataghans, and life is full once more of ortolans and gazelles. Sidonia (whose importance in *Coningsby* has, I think, been overestimated) reappears here to direct *Tancred* to return to the Semitic roots of Christian faith in Palestine. In itself this might seem sound advice, but when Sidonia, a sort of super-Disraeli, who says he knows "the secret history of the world," turns his attention to the "Asian Mystery" and the Secrets of Race we recognize a figure out of the author's romantic past. The secret histories were full of cryptic Goethean mentors pregnant with banalities about romantic individualism and the supremacy of youth. *Tancred* is altogether a very strange book. Running through it is Disraeli's passionate and in its way moving attempt at a grand vindication of the Jews, yet even here the tone is uncertain. The grand finale, involving the noble young English Tancred's marriage to a beautiful Semitic maiden of most ancient lineage, carries, in contrast to the socially and economically significant alliances that terminate *Coningsby* and *Sybil*, only the vaguest kind of meaning, and Disraeli seems to hover between taking the whole thing in deadly earnest and treating it all as an elaborate joke. Possibly lurking within *Tancred* there is not a religious novel, but a diplomatic novel, for Disraeli does attempt in the chaotic later chapters a quite complex confrontation of East and West.

After 1847, Disraeli apparently had resolved Contarini's old dilemma for himself, turning definitively from art to politics, but two more novels were written in periods of respite. *Lothair* (1870), which he wrote in the quiet months following his first brief premiership, suggests more than anything else, self-parody. All the antics are there, the usual hero, the usual setting, the usual educative program, the usual final felicities. But it is a thin performance. The novel again makes some claims to serious intentions, behaving as though it were a profound examination of the spiritual and political conflicts of the age. But in *Lothair* politics are only toyed with. Although it is set in the 1860's the final struggles for Reform are not mentioned, and Irish nationalism is dismissed lightly as a "fairy tale." Spirituality appears only in the shape of Disraeli's perennial dilettante fascination with Catholicism; as for the solemn probings into the soul and its significance for the age, the novel's spasmodic switching from religiosity to frivolity, though sometimes funny, in the end only underlines Disraeli's fundamental uneasiness in these spheres.

Endymion, Disraeli's last complete novel, which he began soon after *Lothair*, laid aside when he became Prime Minister again, and finally published in 1880, once more seems an exercise in self-parody, or self-plagiarism. The narrative follows a Vivian Grey-like young man through the twenties, thirties, and forties, and amounts to a nostalgic review of that epoch. Disraeli here draws on the rich stores of information he had acquired throughout his years of power and influence. The novel is packed with identifiable characters and, of course, has its autobiographical and historical interest. But it is disconcertingly trivial after the major trilogy. The consistent attitude that emerges from all the irony and light sentiment and semi-serious philosophizing is that politics and diplomacy are nothing more than a game—"mankind is my great game"—as Vivian Grey had been made to say fifty years earlier. But some of Vivian's brilliance, as well, of course, as his absurdity, has now disappeared. *Endymion* is a collection of highly informed gossip: self-parody with a vengeance.

Self-parody pervades Disraeli's irony throughout his novels, but like the irony itself it is most meaningful when something more than a game is going on. In

Coningsby and *Sybil* he works through his ironical refinements to achieve a complex self-commitment (as he does not in *Lothair* or *Endymion*), a commitment which is not at odds with his imagination. When Disraeli was working out his romantic subjectivism he was on the whole an uneasy figure. Even in the promising *Contarini Fleming,* for example, his erratic Byronism tends to destroy any real imaginative life, to turn his art into mere pose—self-consciousness falsifying itself. On the other hand what is most impressive about *Coningsby* and *Sybil* is the manner in which Disraeli, even when we have allowed for his romantic extravagances, is able to get beyond subjectivity and to make his idiosyncratic imagination live, make it commit itself, in quite serious moral statement. This was something that so many great mid-Victorians were trying to do. The age, we are now so often told, was full of divided minds and alien visions, of artists striving to channel their private energies into adequate public affirmations while maintaining their artist's integrity. The greatest amongst them have left us some very uneven results; certainly Disraeli's achievement, with all the reservations one must make, does not always suffer in comparison. And if we look for the secret of his success we may find it in his underlying awareness, at even his most serious moments (and in an age that was becoming more and more dedicated to a certain kind of oppressive seriousness) that his great talent was for comedy.

His great talent did not make Disraeli a great novelist. He is not even a great political novelist as is, for example, the genius of *Nostromo* and *Under Western Eyes.* Disraeli does not give us Conrad's rich presentation of political ideas imaginatively lived in terms of immediately realized personalities and relationships. Yet he should be recognized as a serious and original artist. He was serious in his determination to make of the novel something more than artificial entertainment, to make it something intelligently concerned with the spirit of the age. He was original in the inimitable form that he constructed to achieve this aim.

"Nothing is so easy as to laugh," as Disraeli said to those jeering members of Parliament in December, 1837, but as one looks over all the brilliancies and absurdities, the sense and nonsense that make up this closely related yet highly varied series of novels, it is impossible not to be impressed by the achievement as a whole. Behind it all lurks the spirit of that clever and complex man, Benjamin Disraeli, constantly challenging the reader to come to terms with his elusive mind.

MRS. GASKELL
AND "THE SEVERE TRUTH"

Charles Shapiro

ON JULY 9, 1853, Charlotte Brontë took time out from her suffering to pen a note to her good, kind friend Elizabeth Gaskell. The letter began with a shrewd bit of literary advice. "A thought strikes me. Do you, who have so many friends,—so large a circle of acquaintance—find it easy, when you sit down to write, to isolate yourself from all those ties, and their sweet associations, so as to be your *own woman*, uninfluenced or swayed by the consciousness of how your work may affect other minds; what blame or what sympathy it may call forth? Does no luminous cloud ever come between you and the severe Truth, as you know it in your own secret and clear-seeing soul? In a word, are you never tempted to make your characters more amiable than the Life, by the inclination to assimilate your thoughts to the thoughts of those who always *feel* kindly, but sometimes fail to *see* justly? Don't answer the question; it is not intended to be answered."

But two of Mrs. Gaskell's novels do seem to answer Miss Brontë's sharp query. For, in *Mary Barton*, where Mrs. Gaskell writes with a fury, with an intent to correct injustice, something does go very wrong; but in *Cranford*, where the author is very much her own woman, things go very well indeed.

Kathleen Tillotson believes that *Mary Barton*, the

novel that brought instant fame to Mrs. Gaskell, is more than a soapbox polemic, that the fiction "transcends" the " 'condition of England' question." She feels that there is "no patronage or condescension toward suffering." Which, I suppose, is true enough as all the characters who enter, speak, and disappear in the novel, rich and poor alike, are frightful caricatures, grotesques unredeemed by either artistry or wit. And matters are made no better when Mrs. Gaskell tosses in her own little observations. On one occasion her central figure, the much put-upon John Barton, has suffered one of the many rebuffs a rotten society forces on him. Mrs. Gaskell feels she must editorialize. "The actions of the uneducated seem to me typified in those of Frankenstein, that monster of many human qualities, ungifted with a soul, a knowledge of the difference between good and evil." (As all fans of horror films can verify, Frankenstein was the scientist, not the monster.)

The plot itself, obtrusive and naked, for there is not much else to deserve notice, is unbelievably forced and foolish: a plucky young girl goes blind; a fallen woman repents; a decent man is driven to murder; a pretty woman is loved by two men, one poor but honest, the other rich but a rake. And there is dialogue to match. " 'I tell thee I'm not the man for thee,' adding an opprobrious name." The novel of social significance, after all, must begin by being a novel. Otherwise the protagonists become cartoons and any messages the author wishes to deliver, worthy as they might be, can only appear ridiculous.

True, Mrs. Gaskell does make a try. Like so many writers before and after her, she attempts to make the setting reflect the characters; and certainly, in the hands of a master (say Dickens in the beginning of *Bleak House* or in the descriptions of the factory town in *Hard Times*) this is a viable artistic device. But consider the opening of *Mary Barton*. After the reader has been treated to a description of the country outside of Manchester, the *meaning of it all* obtrudes. "I do not know whether it was on a holiday granted by the masters, or a holiday seized in right of Nature and her beautiful spring time by the workmen, but one afternoon (now ten or a dozen years ago) these fields were much thronged." Among those thronging were factory girls who "wore the usual out-of-doors dress of that particular class of maidens; namely a shawl." They appeared as any group of girls might, with one exception. "The only thing to strike a passer-by was an acuteness and intelligence of countenance, which has often been noticed in a manufacturing population."

Over and over Mrs. Gaskell contrasts background with inhabitants. "The next evening there was warm, pattering, incessant rain—just the rain to waken up the flowers. But in Manchester, where, alas! there are no flowers, the rain had only a disheartening and gloomy effect; the streets were wet and dirty, the drippings from the houses were wet and dirty, and the people were wet and dirty. Indeed, most kept within doors; and there was an unusual silence of footsteps in the little paved courts." Epanalepsis has, I am afraid, been used to better effect. And Mrs. Gaskell's attempts at comic description are little improvement. "Houses, sky, people, and everything looked as if a gigantic brush had washed them all over with a dark shade of Indian ink." After the latter quotation the author goes on to tell us that if the poor are dirty it really isn't their own fault, for conditions are not what they should be.

Mrs. Gaskell, having sacrificed all to get her fairly simply messages across to her readers, perhaps deserves to be studied on her own terms. Let us try to see just how her protests come across, how effective her demands for justice are, when couched in literary terms. Our little Miss Muckraker shows no mercy and little understanding. Consider the following exchanges on pages 72 and 8:

"Eh, John! donna talk so; sure there's many and many a master as good or better nor us."

"If you think so, tell me this. How comes it they're rich, and we're poor? I'd like to know that. Han they done as they'd be done by for us?"

"We're their slaves as long as we can work; we pile up their fortunes with the sweat of our brows, and yet we are to live as separate as if we were in two worlds; ay, as separate as Dives and Lazarus, with a great gulf betwixt us."

All the dice are loaded, in description even as in dialogue.

Carson's mill ran lengthways from east to west. Along it went one of the oldest thoroughfares in Manchester. Indeed, all that part of the town was comparatively old; it was there that the first cotton mills were built, and the crowded alleys and back streets of the neighbourhood made a fire there particularly to be dreaded. The staircase of the mill ascended from the entrance at the western end, which faced into a wide, dingy-looking street, consisting principally of public-houses, pawnbrokers' shops, rag and bone warehouses, and dirty provision shops. The other, the east end of the factory, fronted into a very narrow back street, not twenty feet wide, and miserably lighted and paved. Right against this end of the factory were the gable ends of the last house in the principal street—a house which from its size, its handsome stone facings, and the attempt at ornament in the front, had probably been once a gentleman's house; but now the light which streamed from its enlarged front windows made clear the interior of the splendidly fitted up room, with its painted walls, its pillared recesses, its gilded and gorgeous fittings-up, its miserable squalid inmates. It was a gin palace.

When Mrs. Gaskell, forever the crusader, puts in a few personal observations, matters get even worse. We are informed that "there is no religionist so zealous as a convert; no masters so stern, and regardless of the interests of the workpeople, as those who have risen from such a station themselves." And we are ordered to remember "that though it may take much suffering to kill the able-bodied and effective members of society, it does *not* take much to reduce them to worn, listless, diseased creatures, who thenceforward crawl through life with moody hearts and pain-stricken bodies."

Mary Barton is liberally salted with snatches of poems and folksongs, all serving to hammer home an already tiresome argument. One of the humbler protagonists, for example, recites a number of verses from a work by one Samuel Bamford, including the line "His shirtless bosom to the blast is bare" and concluding with "Shall toil and famine, hopeless, still be borne? / No! God will yet arise and help the poor!" And the lovely folksinger, already mentioned as due to go blind, belts out such ditties as "The Oldham Weaver."

> *Oi'm a poor cotton-weyver, as mony a one knoowas*
> *Oi've nowt for t' yeat, an' oi've worn eawt my clooas,*
> *Yo'ad hardly gi' tuppence for aw as oi've on,*
> *My clogs are both brosten, an' stockings oi've none,*
>   *Yo'd think it wur hard,*
>   *To be browt into th' warld,*
> *To be——clemmed, an' do th' best as yo con.*

We are treated to seven more verses of the same, after which one and all of the listeners "had the enjoyment of tears."

The best portions of *Mary Barton* come when Mrs. Gaskell forgets her special pleading and does what she can do so well, observe, with humor, the social habits of her subjects. Her description of the Carson women, wealthy, spoiled but very human, give us some hints of the future joys to be discovered in *Cranford*. Mrs. Carson, newly rich, is seen "Indulging in the luxury of a head-ache. . . . She was not well, certainly. 'Wind in the head,' the servants called it. . . . It would have done her more good than all the ether and salvolatile she was daily in the habit of swallowing, if she might have taken the work of one of her housemaids for a week; made beds, rubbed tables, shaken carpets, and gone out into the fresh morning air without all the paraphernalia of shawl, cloak, boa, fur boots, bonnet, and veil, in which she was equipped before setting out for an 'airing' in the closely-shut carriage."

As for her daughters—they are bored. "One tried to read 'Emerson's essays' and fell asleep in the attempt; the other was turning over a parcel of new songs, in order to select what she liked. Amy, the youngest, was copying some manuscript music. The air was heavy with the fragrance of strongly-scented flowers, which sent out their night odours from an adjoining conservatory." And they prattle on about last night's ball, beaus, and their boredom. The first debutantes are born.

This humor, and a good deal more, carries over into Mrs. Gaskell's best work, *Cranford*. *Cranford*, in a real sense, *is* Mrs. Gaskell, because it is honest, observant, compassionate; and it is her best work because it sees clearly and holds together as an artistic creation. The tone is set right at the outset, announcing themes, proclaiming affection, hinting at soft criticisms. For though some critics see *Cranford* as a collection of assorted tales and episodes united only by a common locale, it is very much a novel in the same way that *Winesburg, Ohio* and *The Dubliners* are more than short story collections.

In the first place, Cranford is in possession of the Amazons; all the holders of houses, above a certain rent, are women. If a married couple come to settle in the town, somehow the gentleman disappears; he is fairly frightened to death by being the only man in the Cranford evening parties, or he is accounted for by being with his regiment, his ship, or closely engaged in

business all the week in the great neighboring community of Drumble, distant only twenty miles on a rail-
road. In short, whatever does become of the gentlemen,
they are not at Cranford. What could they do if they
were there? The surgeon has his round of thirty miles,
and sleeps at Cranford; but every man cannot be a
surgeon. For keeping the trim gardens full of choice
flowers without a weed to speck them; for frightening
away little boys who look wistfully at the said flowers
through the railings; for rushing out at the geese that
occasionally venture into the gardens if the gates are
left open; for deciding all questions of literature and
politics without troubling themselves with unnecessary
reasons or arguments; for obtaining clear and correct
knowledge of everybody's affairs in the parish; for keeping their neat maid-servants in admirable order; for
kindness (somewhat dictatorial) to the poor, and real
tender good offices to each other whenever they are in
distress, the ladies of Cranford are quite sufficient. "A
man," as one of them observed to me once, "is *so* in the
way in the house!" Although the ladies of Cranford
know all each other's proceedings, they are exceedingly
indifferent to each other's opinions. Indeed, as each has
her own individuality, not to say eccentricity, pretty
strongly developed, nothing is so easy as verbal retalia-
tion; but somehow goodwill reigns among them to a
considerable degree.

This opening paragraph prepares us for the delights
ahead and sets the limitations of the action to be
expected. In short, from the first few sentences *Cranford* is an almost perfect little (dare I say "minor")
novel.

Chapter III ("A Love Affair of Long Ago") is typical. Miss Matty, a bumbling, naive, lovable old maid
(and where has that breed gone to?) has suffered the
loss of her older sister, the bossy Miss Jenkyns, and our
narrator pays her a visit to help and comfort. Miss
Matty's first request is that, henceforth, she be addressed as "Matilda," for that was the name her dear
sister preferred. "I promised faithfully . . . and we

all tried to drop the more familiar name, but with so little success that by and by we gave up the attempt." Truth, in important matters, seems to be able to take the measure of the Cranford citizens.

Homely events take place: a new servant, rough but decent, is broken in, a veritable torture for Miss Matty, and a cousin of hers, "who had been twenty or thirty years in India" pays a visit with an invalid wife and two servants. In both cases, confronted with her inferiors as well as her betters, Matty bungles through. Her decency is too much for artificial social barriers. Thus, with constant reminders of her goodness and the long and hard influence of her late strict sister, we are prepared for the revelation that, once in bygone days, Matty truly loved a blunt but iconoclastic gentleman.

This bold chap lived "four or five miles" from Cranford on his tiny estate and one of his quirks was a steadfast refusal to be called "*Esq.*" He would return letters using this term, informing the postmistress at Cranford "that his name was *Mr.* Thomas Holbrook, yeoman." He spoke in a loud voice and we feel he was a fine man. But, as a neighbor commented, Miss Matty did not marry him, though she did love him, for he "would not have been enough of a gentleman for the rector and Miss Jenkyns." Thus, the man who wanted to be called "Mr." and the lady who wanted to be addressed as "Matilda" live out their lives alone. At the end of the chapter Miss Matty meets her old lover while purchasing some silks. Both parties are flustered. "She went straight to her room; and never came back till our early tea-time, when I thought she looked as if she had been crying."

Social criticism is sly and not, as in *Mary Barton*, delivered with a drastic, heavy hand. Two sisters, former ladies' maids, save their money and open up a milliner's shop well patronized by the quality. "They would not sell their caps and ribbons to any one without a pedigree." And many a farmer's wife or daughter, it is reported, was "turned away huffed" from the establishment. More crucial, when the bank in which Miss Matty has her small life savings goes under, the true measure of Cranford is taken. Her rough servant girl contrives to stay with Miss Matty; Miss Matty, herself, behaves admirably and honestly; and her friends, gossips though they might be, help in hidden ways. The episodes surrounding the bank failure are as telling an indictment as the famous chapter in *Dombey and Son* wherein Dickens describes the crash of the house of Dombey and damns Victorian capitalism.

Mrs. Gaskell's strength lies in how well she knows and loves her characters and this, in turn, rests on her femininity, her own qualities as a good woman. Elizabeth Cleghorn Stevenson married early, had seven children, was a devoted wife to her minister husband, cried a good deal and, according to all reports, loved a good gossip. Her portrait shows a pretty woman. David Cecil is undoubtedly correct when he observes that as Trollope was the typical Victorian man, "so Mrs. Gaskell was the typical Victorian woman." Or we can only hope so, considering the weird faces the Brontës and George Eliot presented to the world.

Mrs. Gaskell's gentle biographer, Elizabeth Haldane, has this to say of her subject. "Her life was in no way remarkable. It had no striking event; it led its passive way along what might seem a well-beaten track. . . . Her married life was even and contented. Children were given to her, and she was a model mother."

At the risk of being considered Fiedlerian, I would like to suggest that there are depths to both Mrs. Gaskell and *Cranford* of a Freudian nature, hinted at in the same coy way our authoress hints at social criticism. Consider, for just one more time, the already quoted opening paragraph of the novel. Cranford is described as being "in the possession of the Amazons." Also consider the way reports of marriages, contemplated as well as realized, strike terror into the hearts and souls of these "Amazons" of the town, old maids and widows alike. Then, for a moment, observe the "male" characters who are either elderly and therefore nonsexual or are confirmed in their active bachelorhood. The exception is Matty's prodigal brother who returns from his foreign adventures and does seem a lusty sort. But he returns only as an elderly man. Significantly, he ran away from his parsonage home as a youth after a series of pranks, some of which were of an obvious transvestite nature. The darling of his mother, he loved practical jokes. Miss Matty reports one incident. "He even took my father in once, by dressing himself up as a lady that was passing through the town and wished to see the Rector of Cranford 'who had published that admirable Assize Sermon.'" On another occasion, the minister returns home to find his son, dressed once more as a woman, cavorting around the front lawn to the amusement of the local inhabitants. The result was a flogging; and right after the beating Matty's brother leaves home. This womanly world of Cranford does have its complications.

I would hate to be an authority on Mrs. Gaskell; so much of her work is so bad. But, if truth must out, there have been those who disagree, notably Henry James, and we even have had brave souls who have studied her life, who revere her social and political insights, and who have complimented the worthy lady with close readings of her fiction. James D. Barry, in an essay reviewing Gaskell scholarship, tells us that "the attention given her in recent times is short of what her contemporary fame would lead us to expect," yet Barry does go on to speculate that there will be "useful and exciting investigations" ahead (imagine the thrills awaiting those attending future M.L.A. meetings), that, indeed, there is a need "for an overall critical study of Mrs. Gaskell's fiction and a reassessment of her position both within Victorian fiction and within English fiction as a whole." I doubt it. Let us love *Cranford* and forgive her for the rest. After all, we do know that this lovely book was the only one of hers she cared to reread. As Mrs. Gaskell wrote to no less than Ruskin, "Sometimes when I am ailing or ill I take *Cranford* and I was going to say enjoy it (but that would not be pretty), laugh over it afresh."

ARTHUR MACHEN
AMONG THE ARTHURIANS

Berta Nash

ARTHUR MACHEN, in his own words "the descendant of a long line of Welsh priests," has been classed by a modern scholar with the twentieth-century Arthurians, Charles Williams, T. S. Eliot, C. S. Lewis and T. H. White.[1] He was born at Caerleon-upon-Usk and was acquainted from his earliest years with Welsh landscape and folklore. In addition to becoming acquainted with Tennyson, Spenser, and Malory, he was early trained in medieval lore, spending some time in the British Museum searching out and studying French manuscripts in preparation for a series of articles for the *Academy* on the subject of the Grail.

Until the latter part of the nineteenth century all of the "matter of Britain" was regarded by intellectuals as wholly fictitious, a compound of literary creation and local legend, but the historicity of Arthur is now accepted by most historians. That is, such experts have agreed that there was, about the fifth century A.D., a local Celtic kinglet named Arthur who managed to knit the regional rulers into a loose confederacy which partially succeeded in withstanding the Anglo-Saxon invaders.

King Arthur and his knights, then, are now regarded as reasonably well authenticated, historical or quasihistorical personages. No such shelter, however, is extended to that portion of the story which relates to the quest for the Grail. Such material is still regarded as a product of the natural creativity of the poetic mind acting upon the local legendary materials. To this is perhaps to be added the importance of the Christian church in those centuries, and its emphasis upon relics, miracle-working objects which were the material legacy of Christ and his Saints.

By strictly historical standards then, the tales about Arthur and his knights are supported by some evidence and may be regarded as at least partly factual. The Grail stories, on the other hand, may be separated from the others by the circumstance that they have no such support at present and are usually regarded as wholly legendary.

Curiously enough, Machen's tale "The Great Return" faithfully follows this separation. In it is no word of Arthur, his Round Table, or the quest for the Grail, although Machen utilizes in a large measure fairly well known material associated with King Arthur and his knights. In many ways the tale is only a fragment of the Gospel story in the dress of 1915. The Grail, with its guardians, the three fishermen, visits a little coastal village for a few days. Because of its intervention, a deaf woman hears, a girl at the point of death is healed, unrelenting enemies are reconciled, the wealthy and the poor, the fox and the hound play together, and all Christians, of many different sects, worship together in the Mass of the Sangraal. The return referred to in the title is not the one prophesied for Arthur, but the transient return of the Grail. Machen is an Arthurian without Arthur.

This is unexpected. Machen, when known at all, is known as a Welshman, a romantic, a purveyor of stories of horror, and—occasionally—as an Arthurian. None of this applies to "The Great Return." It may be objected that this tale is late and untypical. Perhaps so, but I am still curious about it. This one story has been held sufficiently significant to class Machen with a group of important writers of this century.

Machen knew the Arthurian stories well. The

Welsh history and landscape are used not only in his *Hill of Dreams*, but in his shorter works also. However, none of his tales is about a leader, or about any society or group. Whatever his interests may have been, he was not occupied in his writing with man in the mass. He deals with the individual, and his individuals are frequently lonely and isolated. So it is in "The Great Return." There is not only no Arthur; there is no other hero either. There is an object—the Grail; there are a series of events—its manifestations; but there is no attempt to delineate or develop a character. This seems to be true in many of Machen's tales. He describes a circumstance or chronicles a series of events, traces the causes, but allows no one a dominant role. Rather he frequently uses an objective bystander, a reporter who describes the events as they occur, but who does not involve himself in the action. In this respect at least, "The Great Return" is typically Machen.

In other ways, too, the story may be more typical of Machen than it first seems, in that it brings together—though in uncharacteristic fashion—his characteristic themes. It is mystic, supernatural, as are many of Machen's better-known tales—for example, "The Novel of the Black Seal," "The White Powder," "The Shining Pyramid," "The Great God Pan," "The Terror." But these are tales of evil and horror, whereas "The Great Return" is a tale of joy.[2] It is, however, a tale of joy which perhaps can be read as symbolizing, fairly late in Machen's career, a kind of solution, or resolution, of the sharp dichotomy between the material and the spiritual world which underlies the tales of horror. But before we speak of the resolution symbolized in "The Great Return" we must first speak of what it is that causes the horror in the tales of horror.

Machen is often painted as a romantic escapist. It is true that in his early years he was well trained in the medieval and the occult; as a native of Caerleon he came early and naturally to the landscape and legend of Wales. As a writer who came of age at a time when the fashionable scene included homosexuality, Satanism, spiritualism and other dabblings of a dubious nature, he became aware of the multifarious human traffic ostensibly forbidden in "polite" society. His own inclinations, his background, his education, the current popularity of the supernatural, teamed with the economic pressure upon him—all helped him along the pathway he had chosen.

In the early horror stories "The Great God Pan" and "The Novel of the White Powder," the series of events is initiated respectively by a surgical manipulation and by a prescription, both the work of physicians —the one performing knowingly, the other innocently. In these tales are manifested, perhaps consciously, the already conventional opposition between the scientist and the spiritualist, the materialist and the seeker after the invisible, the imponderable, the immeasurable. At first glance it would seem that Machen is fighting on the side of the angels and is wholeheartedly opposed to the scientific materialist. Actually, however, Machen does not oppose the material per se, but seeks a reconciliation of natural and supernatural. In providing a material, scientifically verifiable means for achieving his end, he thus works to construct a bridge connecting the opposing angry cliffs. In "The White Powder," Dr. Chambers says, "The whole universe . . . is a tremendous sacrament . . . and man, and the sun, and the other stars, and the flower of the grass, and the crystal in the test-tube are each and every one as spiritual, as material. . . ." [3]

"The Novel of the Black Seal" first appears in the book which also contains "The Novel of the White Powder." In this tale supernatural manifestations are produced by pronouncing a formula, the iteration of certain words in an ancient tongue in a prescribed form and manner. Such a procedure is, of course, nearer to the studies of a "social" scientist, an archaeologist or philologist, than to those of an "exact" scientist, a surgeon or a chemist. It is also, by the way, consonant with the magic and the Rosicrucian incantations that he learned later.

Indeed, throughout much of Machen's writing is the idea that men are composed of two disparate elements. Contrary to much contemporary opinion, he does not suggest that man is a material being and also a rational intellect, with a third part (usually called the spirit or soul) which somehow manages the pair. He does not try to say that the physical is wholly representative of evil while the spiritual element symbolizes the good. These elements are never to be considered as irreconcilable opposites, but as typifying that diversity in unity which is humanity at its most noble.

The tales of horror, of evil, are nearly all occult and supernatural; they are also nearly all stories in which an immaterial evil prevails over a balanced human being because of the use of some material agency. In tale after tale horror prevails because of some effort made which destroyed that delicate balance. Indeed it would appear that the greatest depth of evil to which man can descend is to effect a separation between the physical and the spiritual in the human creature. Dr. Chambers writes, "The house of life was riven asunder and the human trinity dissolved. . . . and for so terrible an act as this, in which the very inmost place of the temple was broken open . . . a terrible vengeance followed." [4] In *The Inmost Light* Dr. Black writes: "From some human being there must be drawn that essence which men call the soul." [5] And in *The Great God Pan* Dr. Raymond confesses that he too "broke open the door of the house of life." [6]

One of the effects of such balanced men is described in a tale composed somewhat later, *The Terror*, where Machen writes of the proper relationship between man and the lesser animals,

> the spiritual has reigned over the rational through the peculiar quality and grace of spirituality that men possess that makes a man to be that which he is. . . .

There was supremacy on the one hand, and submission on the other; but at the same time there was between the two that cordiality which exists between lords and subjects in a well-organized state.[7]

In view of that passage one perceives why it is that in the earlier tales of evil the consequence of cleaving asunder the "house of life" is always a "reversion" to the animal, in which the victim descends again the scale of evolution as Dr. Matheson describes it in *The Great God Pan*.

Here too was all the work by which man had been made repeated before my eyes. I saw the form waver from sex to sex, dividing itself from itself, and then again reunited. Then I saw the body descend to the beasts whence it ascended, and that which was on the heights go down to the depths, even to the abyss of all being.[8]

In one sense, perhaps, the "putrid mass" which was the last stage of Francis Leicester of "The White Powder" may be likened to Poe's "nearly liquid mass of loathsome—of detestable putridity" [9]; in another sense, one may regard it as the primal ooze—a rather different thing.

Machen's reputation as a purveyor of the occult and the horrible depends in part upon the fact that these are tales of complete corruption. Their blackness is unrelieved. A human being, however, would never serve as a villain for such a story, for, according to Machen's theory, no human creature is capable of such entire and unrestrained evil. Although Machen was, in an earlier period, well dosed with medieval manuscripts, he does not use demons, fallen angels, in this role even though he is occupied with a supernatural story. What he requires is a wholeheartedly wicked being, superficially human but without any divine admixture—soulless. Finding no such race of creatures in the universe, he does what any creative writer would do in such an emergency. He invents one.

Essentially his myth starts with the wholly logical supposition that the British Isles were home to a different race before the advent of the Celt. With the coming of the Celtic tribes these beings neither departed nor were assimilated by the invaders; they went underground. To this day these troglodytes live on in the caves and hills of Cornwall and Wales. Their presence is not, of course, completely unknown. With a kind of propitiation for the hostile forces which they represent, and with the kind of instinct displayed by other peoples in like emergencies, the country folk refer to them in folk tale, ballad and literature as the "little people," "fays," "fairies," "the good people."

Reynolds and Charlton have asserted that Machen did not believe this stuff, that he invented it for the sole benefit of his character, Professor Gregg.[10] I do not think that it is germane here to know all that Machen came to believe or disbelieve, nor do I doubt that much of this legend was initiated as he developed the figure of Professor Gregg for *The Novel of the Black Seal.* Machen continued and elaborated the myth, however, in other tales. In *The Black Seal* these survivals are ancient stone-age creatures, speaking "a jargon but little removed from the inarticulate noises of brute beasts." [11] Although Machen describes them as primitive, they have developed a cuneiform-like writing. They have singular customs as well as peculiar powers of transmuting themselves.

These creatures appear again in "The Shining Pyramid," where Machen refers to "the very probable belief that they represent a tradition of the prehistoric Turanian inhabitants of the country, who were cave-dwellers." [12] The basic approach is the same. The country folk call them fairies. They are stone-age troglodytes who communicate by pictures made with an arrangement of flint arrowheads. They "seemed to speak to one another in . . . tones of horrible sibilance." Machen emphasizes their short stature, their Mongolian features, and the reports that they are soulless. These "little people" appear prominently in the later tale "Out of the Earth," and are referred to in "The Terror." Perhaps Machen was already manufacturing and recombining the elements of this legend when he wrote, in a tale composed earlier in his career ("The White People," 1906), "and in the Middle Ages the followers of a very old tradition had known how to use it for their own purposes." [13] Thus Machen creates an evil element for his tales of horror which represents the material wholly purged of any spiritual admixture. These creatures are not only evil; they are soulless. They are inhuman, and are not even animals. Animals at least are capable of evolving into higher forms but these have no such promise.

Such are the tales of horror; stories in which individuals sometimes accidentally, sometimes deliberately, so overturn the natural balance of a human creature that there occurs an unnatural separation of the elements which form its composition. *The Hill of Dreams*, although longer and more involved than most of Machen's work, belongs, throughout most of its length, to this group. In the tales which he wrote in his later years the apparently supernatural visions or visitations seemed to occur spontaneously, as in "The Happy Children" the supernatural benefits seem to fall upon the recipients by chance, certainly through no intervention of their own. The winds of the spirit, whether malevolent or benevolent, blow when and on whom they will, without the need of any material agency or the directions of any external power.

Perhaps a detailed look at one of the "tales of joy" will help us to understand this opposition of horror and joy. In *The Great Return* the supernatural visitation comes unbidden but through the medium of a material utensil, the Grail, and in this story the rite of the Sangraal occurs. This rite, which is celebrated somewhat differently in different Grail stories, is reported in Machen's tale with some special emphases.

It occurs, as in Charles Williams' novelised version, in an old Anglican church. For Machen this arrangement seems to obtain because he thus reverts to a period when one church and one branch of Christianity served the whole region. Whether you call this church Anglican or Roman seems to matter little: it is the church of the three saints, visited by the three holy fishermen.

One of them bears a bell, Teilo Sant, which "had sailed across the glassy seas from Syon," whose wondrous ringing sounds often in the tale. Machen also refers to Capo Teilo, or Chapel Head, where "the old grey chapel of St. Teilo stands." Now during the Roman occupation of Wales (and Caerleon is the site of Isca, of the Legions), Christianity was introduced. When the rest of the land was overrun by the pagan Saxons, Wales was visited by Irish missionaries, among them St. Teilo. No reference to a prediction of the return of the great bell, the bell of St. Teilo, seems to occur in either Malory or the medieval French sources. I am tempted to believe that it is either Machen's invention or was derived by him from some obscure local legend.

The church building itself is unusual in that it preserves, according to a custom still prevailing in the East, an architectural separation between the nave and the chancel, thus maintaining the secrecy to the mysteries celebrated in the course of the Mass. Machen also seems to be using the Great Entrance, still important in the Eastern Rite but unused for many centuries in the westernized churches. The red vesture of the fishermen may echo *de vermeil samit* of one of Malory's French sources, with which the Grail was veiled. Malory's "table of silver" is in Machen the "portable altar" called "Sapphirus," which Machen ascribes to William of Malmesbury, and which

> was like a great jewel, and it was of a blue colour, and there were rivers of silver and of gold running through it and flowing as quick streams flow, and there were

pools in it as if violets had been poured out into water,
and then it was green as the sea near the shore, and
then it was the sky at night with all the stars shining,
and then the sun and the moon came down and washed
in it.[14]

The portable altar seems to have been for some centuries now a utensil used exclusively by the Roman
Catholic Church.

The recurring sound of the great bell speaks at
different times during the Mass of the Sangraal, since
Machen also uses it as the still widely heard sanctus or
sacring bell, the bell which is used in some Anglican
and Roman Catholic churches to alert the worship-
pers to especially sacred parts of the service. In some
early texts it is called the saint's bell. One passage in
this tale, however, seems to indicate that Machen is
here following the eastern practice of ringing the bell
in the tower at one point to announce to the neigh-
borhood that the consecration has been completed.[15]

The tongues which Machen employ form a curious
mixture of Greek, Welsh, and Latin. Though much of
the rite seems to be borrowed, like the architecture,
from an earlier tradition, the spontaneous interjec-
tions and the use of a Wesleyan hymn imply a combination with more recent elements, so that the "return" of the title is not just a regression to more
antique practices, but a return to a union of diverse
elements, a unity of the sons of God.

The Mass of the Holy Grail, moreover, is attended
by different groups in different tales, usually by a small
exclusive group, selected upon the principles which
the author of the tale deems appropriate. In *The
Great Return* the congregation occupies every seat,
fills all the aisles and flows into the churchyard.
Machen deliberately submerges all sectarian differences
in the worship of the Grail. As he writes, "There was
not a single chapel of the Dissenters open . . . that
day. The Methodists . . . and all the Non-conform-
ists had returned on this Sunday morning to 'the old
hive.' " [16]

For Machen this conception comes quite naturally. To him, apparently, a communion is inherently a union of different parts, in which the human merges with the divine without either one losing any of its special qualities. Scholars have expanded considerable energy over whether the Grail was chalice or paten, or perhaps now one, now the other—depending on what time and place was then creating its contribution to the legend—but neither Machen nor anyone else of his religious persuasion would give the subject any serious thought. For Machen, as for many another, the Mass, the Eucharist, the Holy Communion, the "breaking of bread"—call it what you will—*is* "the body of Christ, which is given for you" and the elements of it can no more be separated than Shylock was able to exact his pound of flesh without carrying off some of the blood. By the same token, the holy vessel may be—and has been—bowl, cup, or both. Furthermore, whether in a human body or not, if the cup is there, Christ is there. The works in which the presence of the cup or bell seems to be the agent parallel the biblical accounts of the deeds of Christ. For Machen, then, the Grail is not only an interesting literary legend of respectable antiquity, it is also a symbol of the Christian teaching, a symbol which possesses the special power of becoming that which it represents.

Why, you may ask, all this to-do over *The Great Return?* Few people consider it his greatest work; other compositions must be contemplated if we are examining literary merit, among them *The Hill of Dreams.* It is not his last word; he wrote subsequently, and, like his earlier writings, the later works are tales of phantasy and terror. It is not even about Arthur.

Perhaps others have found different answers, but for me *The Great Return* has led to a kind of insight into the nature of Machen's writings. At first it seemed a pleasant tale, but as I read more of his work I became aware of the curious dichotomy of his moods. His tales are either unutterably horrible or completely joyous. He knows no middle way. Initially I accepted him as a typical product of his time, an age of conflict between the scientist and the humanist, the good mystic opposed to the evil materialist.

However, the Grail for him is not spiritual but material, and furthermore he appears to be at some pains to establish the reality of the old woman's deafness, the illness of the girl, the enmity of the men. Furthermore, it appears that in the tales of horror, although the evil is initiated by a physical agency, it invariably culminates in a complete corruption. Even though the spirit is eliminated the material remainder is also dissolved, for no single element in the human compound may exist unsupported by the others. These stories are stories of diminution, in which a person is destroyed in an attempt to separate out an element which is an essential part of him. The other part of the canon, the happier tales, are sums in addition. The actors remain very human and alive. They are recognizable but changed.

For many readers, then, the Grail becomes a symbol of mankind as mankind ought to be, an indissoluble compound of elements. The beginner in chemistry learns that the element chlorine is a gas which is apt to scatter and disappear when exposed to the air; concentrated in large quantities, it becomes poisonous. The element sodium is also hard to isolate, being likely to disappear in a burst of flame, perhaps burning your fingers in the process. In combination these elements become the savoury, ubiquitous, and useful compound—salt. Thus the whole is something very different from the collection of parts which compose it. Evidently, in Machen's view, the human being is such another compound: infinitely various, capable of additions and elaborations, but to be analysed, dissected, and diminished only at the gravest peril.

CHARLES WILLIAMS

Frederick S. Wandall

THE LATE Charles Williams is the author of seven novels and some thirty other books on such subjects as poetry, drama, biography, witchcraft and theology. Though relatively unknown to the public, he was highly regarded in the field of literature by such persons as C. S. Lewis, T. S. Eliot and Dorothy Sayers. As a writer of Christian allegory Williams stands almost alone in this century. The ethical and religious content of the novels may be most baffling to readers and on this I will focus our attention since it was religious ideas that Williams was trying to convey in the most fascinating way he could contrive. Theology—dogmas, doctrines, creeds of the historical Christian church— was not a dull, dry thing to him; it lived and breathed with the energy of reality. Plays, novels, and poems seemed to him the best mediums for explaining (or expounding) theology. Only the reader can decide if he was successful.

Charles Walter Stansby Williams was born September 20, 1886, of cockney origins, educated at St. Alban's School and the University College, London. In 1908 he became an editor of the Oxford University Press, a position he held until his death, May 15, 1945. He married Michal Conway in 1917, and they had one son.

He was a devoted and practicing Christian, a saint to his friends, the leader of a few intellectuals who met monthly in an Oxford pub for long conversations.[1] He was well-read in literature and theology, a lecturer in Oxford University, and an author whose interests ranged from Plato to King Arthur and the Grail, from Dante to the Elizabethans, from country vicars and towns to life in London. He wrote to ease his financial situation; some books are potboilers. But his novels and poems and literary essays are well-done and have acquired an appreciative audience.

There is unity between the man and his books. The seven novels, written between 1930 and 1945, reflect his personality, his wit, his sensitive awareness of the conflict between good and evil, his intense faith, his love and understanding of people. His novels are studies in the varieties of religious experience, but they are more than that. By the use of myth symbolism, the merging of past and present, the coexistence of natural and supernatural events, the use of the stream of consciousness technique and the allegorical method Williams created complex and vivid works of fiction, designed to catch and hold our attention with a good story while presenting the beliefs of Christianity. He did not write solely to entertain. He wrote to give us some idea of the glory and reality of God, the problem of sin and salvation, and the struggle of men and women faced with the choice between good and evil. He lived and wrote in two worlds—the natural and the supernatural—and to him these were contiguous, coinherent and compatible.

As an apologist for Christianity, Williams took his stand upon the orthodox creeds of the Church of England. His interest in theology was profound and expressed itself in books about church history (*The Descent of the Dove*), the incarnation (*He Came Down from Heaven*), and the love of God and man

(*The Figure of Beatrice* and *The Forgiveness of Sins*). Throughout his novels these and other doctrines are given full expression. He speaks of the Fall as the experience of seeing good as evil, the Incarnation as "the Way of the Affirmation of Images," the Redemption as the restoration of the good by the surrender of the will and the acceptance of judgment, the Atonement as the efficacy of substituted love, and the Communion of Saints as the mutual coinherence of all men within the Divine Unity. He thus treats traditional dogmas in unconventional ways, making ancient truths take on new and searching reality. He was convinced that the whole universe is good, because God created it, but he felt with great anguish the pain and suffering in it. It was the work of love to change evil into good, suffering into joy. Only through a deep, thorough commitment to God through Christ and the Holy Spirit could one do this work.

Dante could assume that his readers would know and accept the Church's teaching about sin, penance, conversion, and redemption; Spenser and Milton could also assume some knowledge of and belief in Christian ideas among their readers. In our day the average reader no longer thinks in these terms or feels comfortable with the supernatural. Christianity is largely an empirical religion in America, concerned with "practical" results, business methods, buildings and growth statistics. Both Catholicism and Protestantism are undergoing radical changes in concepts and organization. For the most part Williams' novels will be read and enjoyed by only a limited number who accept and practice Christianity, who believe the articles of the Creeds and who regard theology as a valid field of inquiry and thought. The world of the novels is largely a medieval one, albeit set in our time, where miracles occur, where the supernatural world invades the natural, and where God reigns. If the reader can accept these ideas, the novels will reward him.

We may divide the novels into two groups, the five earlier one written between 1930–33 and the two later novels written in 1937 and 1945. This division is not arbitrary. In the earlier novels, Williams concentrates more on narrative action in the physical world. *War in Heaven* (1930), *Many Dimensions* (1931), and *The Greater Trumps* (1932) make use of objects of supernatural power (respectively the Holy Grail, a jewel from the crown of King Solomon, the Tarot cards) to create a moral crisis in which the characters have to choose whether they will join the forces of good or evil. In *The Place of the Lion* (1931) Platonic ideas are unleashed by human wilfulness and only by the Grace of God is mankind saved. Williams began to turn away from such archetypal images in his next book, *Shadows of Ecstasy* (1933) to concentrate more on the inner warfare of the soul. The two later novels are more complex. *Descent into Hell* (1937) deals with the theology of substituted love ("bearing one another's burdens"), St. Paul's interpretation of the atoning work of Christ applied to the Christian community. The book employs some Joycean techniques in its study of the soul and subconscious mind. *All Hallows' Eve* (1945), published six months before the author's death, is considered by many to be his finest work. It is notable for its presentation of life after death and the growth of love between a woman who is dead and her husband who lives in this world.

On the strictly narrative level these tales seem highly improbable. Whereas Bunyan's allegory is believable because the scenes and events are almost wholly naturalistic, the Williams novels incorporate magic, myth and metaphysics in ways that may leave readers puzzled. Even convinced Christians find difficulty in accepting this medieval frame of mind; perhaps it is one we should try to regain. Yet the miracles and magic were only meant to intrigue the reader and to create a story; they are, it seems to me, actually incidental to the moral or religious problem of choos-

ing between good and evil. As noted, Williams became more and more concerned with the spiritual
nature and development of his characters and less
with magical objects and supernatural invasions of
earthly time and place. The real miracle for Williams
is that man has the freedom and will to discover God
and "enjoy him forever."

The method that Williams used to convey his ideas
was allegory, defined by Miss Drew as "the presentation of experience in symbolic form." [2] This is "the
method of perceiving inner realities *through* their reflection in concrete image." [3] The characters of the
novels are symbolic images introducing us to the inner
realities of life. As in the case of the allegories by
Spenser and Bunyan, the novels move on two levels,
the narrative level, with its natural settings and characterizations, and the moral level with the people symbolizing virtues, vices, ideas, etc. In an allegory, even
events can be symbolic. Williams felt that his characters should be as intensely themselves as possible in
order that the dominant quality of their lives would
be conveyed convincingly. He came remarkably close
to his goal. His characters are well differentiated, with
idiosyncrasies, ideas, speech patterns of their own.
Some are amusing, some pathetic, some noble, others
baffling or contemptible or evil. Like some figures in
Pilgrim's Progress or *The Faerie Queen*, they are not
easily forgotten.

The central problem in each book is that of good
and evil. The characters are brought face to face with
this issue and compelled to make a choice which will
lead ultimately to salvation or damnation. In some
cases the impending destruction of the world is barely
averted by the proper action of those who love God.
This choice is not simply an ethical matter among
human beings; it is a cosmic one involving the Creator
and the forces of evil. We must either be for goodness
(and God) or against it (and Him). But this stark
dichotomy, so bluntly stated here, should not obscure

the complexity of Williams' characters nor the important fact of their freedom to act as they choose. More than any other fact, this emphasis on the *freedom of the will* distinguishes Williams from other allegorical writers. His characters are not narrowly identified with a certain virtue or vice or an institution (e.g., the Church). There may be several ways of categorizing a given character, and this complexity, true to life, adds lustre to the narrative.

A plot summary of each novel would not only exceed the limits imposed on this chapter but also would fail to convey the author's intentions and ideas. A more valuable procedure, perhaps, would be to describe the characters and group them according to their natures.

The range of Williams' characters runs the gamut from evil to beatific; they represent all shades of ethical persuasion, all modes of existence from heaven to hell. It is to Williams' credit that he does not restrict himself to the two extremes of morality or immorality, religious belief or unbelief. The diversity of his allegorical figures is remarkable. All types of people fill the pages of his seven novels: publisher, judge, secretary, priest, historian, professor, African chieftain, artist, old lady, young girls both dead and alive. Each person is a symbolic image of some ethical or religious condition. No two are exactly alike in their beliefs though they may be put into broad categories. They have, on the whole, the vitality, credibility, consistency and intelligibility which are essential in fictional characterization.[4] They have individuality in speech, dress, mannerism, personality. Yet they also fulfill their allegorical function at the same time by *what* they say and *how* they act and think in a given situation. The balance, of course, is difficult to maintain; we can see by the record how few authors have succeeded in the art of allegory, whose purpose is to offer the reader a clearer, deeper knowledge of eternal truths.

These truths, then, are embodied in Williams' characterization. The persons of evil show us a way of life that is frightening in its depravity and hopelessness. On the lowest rung we have such fiends as Simon the Clerk, Gregory Persimmons, Sir Giles Tumulty, and Lily Sammile (Lilith). Their only satisfaction in life is to destroy or dominate others, either by refined necromancy, black magic, perverted science, or psychological persuasion. The latter methods are especially diabolical because they are actual facts, available to all, whereas magic is but a fantastic invention which Williams uses to symbolize the follies men pursue. Sir Giles, Gregory, and Simon seek unlimited and unlawful power over the people of this world and the next. Their minds are so cold and calculating that they seem actually devilish. Like Milton's Satan they glory in their power and evil. Yet it is a sad sight, for they are only human and perforce must meet the damnation common to men of ill will. The end of their careers is appropriate to the way they have lived. In *All Hallows' Eve* Simon's last earthly moments are tormented by his (Platonic) types; his hate and fear are embodied in the magical images (or devils) he has created and they return to destroy him, deflected by the power of love and the Image of the City. He is drawn down into a rose that smells of blood, an ironic damnation for a man who has schooled himself in the most subtle and refined sorts of disciplines in order to gain the knowledge by which he could kill, or make parasites of, whomever he pleased.

Giles Tumulty, in *Many Dimensions,* employs science rather than magic to gain his objectives. His blasphemy of the sacred Stone of Solomon (with the Tretragrammaton of the Holy Name of God) results in its enveloping him (as the rose did Simon), pulling him past memory and desire into a nether world, an eternal void. The use of his reason, which he had perverted, is taken from him. He has chosen the wrong way to knowledge, whereas Chloe (the secretary to the Lord Chief Justice of England), in submission to the divine will, discovers what true wisdom is in the presence of God's Omniscience. Gregory Persimmons (of *War in Heaven*) repents at the last minute, surrenders to the police and prepares to meet whatever fate his Creator has in store. He has already been punished, as Prester John explains, for he has discovered the destruction he wrought, and it is his own.

Less sinister than these, but still seekers of ungodly and sinister powers are Berringer and his cohorts Foster and Wilmot in *The Place of the Lion*, men who wish to unleash the universal powers (the Platonic ideas) without the necessary accompanying ethical or religious and intellectual disciplines. Their destruction by these raw, untamed energies is not surprising. Another perverter of truth is Nigel Considine (from *Shadows of Ecstasy*), the false prophet of immortality and illicit, sinful rapture, whose suave, enticing proclamations lure foolish souls like Roger and Nielsen to his lair and drag them down to disillusion and despair. Considine tries to prolong his life by rejecting natural bodily functions (sex, food, sleep) and living ascetically. This distortion and denial of life, carried to the extreme, is blasphemous. It seeks powers and privileges that belong only to God. The descent into hell becomes inevitable for these men only because they have ignored the warnings to abandon their sinful practices and be born again into a holy life. Reason fails them, their consciences die, their hearts are hardened—and they are lost.

A slightly lesser degree of perversion is seen in the Lee family of *The Greater Trumps*. Henry Lee lusts for the creative powers that reside in the Tarot cards; Aaron Lee for the secret of the universe they may reveal; Joanna Lee for her dead child and her faithless husband. They almost meet death in their mad quests, for Henry and Aaron unleash elemental powers belonging to the cards in order to kill the owner of the Greater Trumps. They are saved by Nancy's love, represented among the cards by the Fool, which controls all the others. The Lees are converted, finding real truth and understanding, as well as the "peace of God, which passeth all understanding."

We need separate classification for Inkamasi, the Zulu king converted to Christianity in *Shadows of Ecstasy*. He is similar to Joanna in that he is a converted pagan. Unable to stand alone in the face of Considine's power in Africa, he succumbs to the hypnotic rhetoric of the High Executive. Caithness, the priest, saves him once from Nigel's clutches, but he is only one man against a superior force of evil. Inkamasi ultimately chooses to die for his faith and royal calling rather than deny either. He thus joins Chloe and the Archdeacon as martyrs to the faith.

The next category may be called "disillusionment," or more accurately, "the life of illusions." Mr. Tighe (in *The Place of the Lion*), Wentworth (in *Descent into Hell*) and Evelyn Mercer (in *All Hallows' Eve*) find actual life disillusioning and turn to their own make-believe world. They reject real people and events—*facts* (so Williams tells us) which are essential to life, for only facts, embodied and concrete, can communicate ideas human and divine. Tighe searches for beauty in butterflies and, finding one gigantic specimen—again a symbol of a Platonic Idea—dies adoring it. Wentworth is frustrated in his desires to obtain Adela Hunt and to prove a rival historian wrong; he finds in a dream the pleasure and pride he cannot have in real life. Slowly he makes the descent into hell, sliding down a rope into insanity, refusing all efforts to save him. It is a hell of silence and emptiness, the opposite pole of the heavenly life. Here Williams is stressing the point that we need companionship both human and divine; we need love and someone to bear our burdens. Evelyn Mercer has never learned that fact. Already a spirit in purgatory, she seeks pity and comfort only for herself. She is driven into the lonely reaches of the City of the Dead, where no voices sound, no people walk. In the end she has only herself.

A bit higher on our scale of values are Quentin Sabot (*The Place of the Lion*), Roger Ingram (*Shadows*), and Lady Wallingford (*All Hallows' Eve*). The predominate characteristic of each is selfishness. Quentin resembles Spenser's Sansfoy in his faithlessness. He does not actively attack goodness, but neither does he defend it: he crumbles at the first blow. He has no defense against the fierce onslaught of reason and demonic energy as manifested in the lion. In servile fear he tries to hide from his enemies, escaping only because Damaris protects him with love and Anthony replaces fear with friendship and authority. Roger Ingram falls prey to Considine's absurd promises of the power of poetry. He, the romantic idealist, the mystic of poetic experience, is emotionally swept away from the city of London (and all it signifies in terms of human life, love and suffering, and possible salvation), away from wife and friends, swept out to sea in a submarine, as a captive of a false prophet, a false god whose death brings him despair. Lady Wallingford comes under the spell of a similar spellbinder, Simon; only at his death is she released from a life of fear and illusion.

On a much higher ethical and intellectual level is a group we shall refer to as rationalists. Williams understood this type of person, skeptical yet willing to accept religion if it is reasonable. The novels contain many examples of such persons. Kenneth Mornington (*War in Heaven*) comes at last to accept the existence of the Holy Grail through his studies of the Arthurian legend. Lord Arglay (*Many Dimensions*) finds religious faith through knowledge of the Stone of Solomon. Damaris Tighe (*The Place of the Lion*) is a scholar; her studies are her idols, separating her from her father and Anthony, almost overpowering her. Yet when Anthony instructs her in the way of love and wisdom, she is able to direct her life towards creative ends and put her studies in perspective.

Three figures possess both reason and faith. Anthony Durrant (*The Place of the Lion*), saviour of Damaris and subduer of the (Platonic) beasts, is wise in the ways of men, humble in the sight of God. The Vicar from *Shadows of Ecstasy*, Ian Caithness, through the sacraments of the Church, is able to foil the ecstatic hypnosis that Considine casts over Inkamasi. He is Roger's spiritual advisor and Considine's adversary. Peter Stanhope (a pseudonym for Williams) [5] is a layman in *Descent into Hell*, a poet who takes Pauline's burden of sin in an exchange of love that leads to her salvation.

An important group is one we shall call "pilgrims" —Chloe Burnett, Nancy Coningsby, Pauline Anstruther, Lester Furnival, Betty Wallingford. They all begin their progress in religion under handicaps of anxiety, frustration, and insufficient spiritual knowledge to meet life's problems. Gradually they learn divine wisdom, the efficacy of love, the rich rewards of a life in God's hands, under the Protection or Omnipotence which guards them. Through them others are saved. All the "pilgrims" are women. All the evil characters are men. For some reason, Williams regarded this situation as the way things happen; he does not explain it.

One more division yet remains. To this belong the saints, so far as we have the right to call the uncanonized in fiction by that name. Saintliness describes the character of the Archdeacon (*War in Heaven*), Sybil Coningsby (*The Greater Trumps*), and Margaret Anstruther (*Descent into Hell*). These are holy people. Reason and faith are in them and more, the beauty of love, humility, patience, and joy. They combine the rarely united qualities of activity and contemplation that lift them above the affairs of ordinary men and women, yet allow them to work wonders in God's name in the world. On their shoulders falls the task of guiding the pilgrims or doing whatever is required to set aside evil. They know the way of God and nothing separates them from Him, not a Gregory Persimmons, or a magically conjured snowstorm or the encroachment of the dead from Gomorrah.

The characters we have reviewed are examples of various religious or nonreligious states of being. Williams was sensitive to the varieties possible to men. Moreover he could translate the psychological or spiritual conditions of man into words that help us understand those conditions better. His comprehension of the nature of man and God and their interrelationship, or lack of it, is profound.

Williams faced the problem of every apologist for Christianity since St. Paul, the problem of making the truths of God (revealed in Scripture, stated in the Creeds and theology of the Church) known to and understood and accepted by a skeptical and worldly minded people. To think in terms of Christian categories, of sin and salvation, of Incarnation and Redemption, to accept Christian moral standards, sacraments, miracles, and the doctrines and Bible of the Church is difficult for modern man who is confronted by the powers of secularization and secularism.[6] An evangelist or apologist must divide the world into two camps, believers and nonbelievers. "Either one is a Christian or one is not. That is to say, the claim of Christianity to be, in the form in which it is set out, with its historical basis a final revelation of the nature of the universe, is in the last resort one which one must either accept or reject. There is no possible compromise." [7] It is the necessity, and joy, of making a choice on the Christian side that confronts a reader of Williams' novels. Not to choose the Christian way of life is to choose a lesser, perhaps a fatally destructive form of existence.

The seven novels have this purpose: to make the modern mind see the urgency and value of a religious faith, a faith that is not fuzzy or semihumanistic, but clearly defined, historically verified, catholic in scope, redemptive in action. We either choose life with God or life without Him, and we make the decision every moment of our lives, in every act and thought. Heaven and Hell are at our doorstep, the world of good and evil extends from time to eternity, and we belong to one or the other as we will. The city we see is but the type of the Divine City, the earthly image of the heavenly City of God. The supernatural world and its inhabitants impinge on our natural world and merge with it; one belongs to the other. So Williams tells us in his novels, plays, and poems.

Contemporary readers of these novels, unless they are students of theology and folklore, may not be convinced by Williams' argument nor understand his stories. He demands faith and knowledge of his readers. Yet for those who will grant him the validity of his premises he is rewarding. He writes for our generation, in idiom we know, about people with problems like ours, relating Christianity to modern needs and circumstances. In the company of C. S. Lewis, T. S. Eliot, W. H. Auden, Grahame Green, Alan Paton, and Christopher Fry, he has worked to continue the Christian message that runs like a thread through English letters from Caedmon to Chaucer to William Golding. By his use of allegory and symbolism Williams kept alive a technique that had all but died; only George MacDonald in our time had given it attention. Although he took the chance of reaching fewer readers by using allegory, it enabled him to bring together the natural and the supernatural, men and spirits, the forces of good and evil, in a realistic fashion. This imaginative fiction opens our eyes to another dimension of life, revealing many psychological and spiritual truths by which we may enrich our lives. We enter another area of being, the world of poetry, imagery, symbols, where truth and knowledge speak to the heart and mind.

Quite probably Williams did not believe in, or expect us to believe in, the existence of the Grail, Solo-

mon's Stone, or Tarot cards, though he had a keen
interest in things occult and mysterious and considered witchcraft a serious threat to Christianity. What
he did expect us to believe is that there is a spiritual
reality, a suprahuman dimension, that links us to all
men and to God, a Reality that finite human reason
cannot hope to penetrate fully, but a Reality which
we know through the images and truths of Christianity. In the discovery of this truth, we find joy and self-
realization.

What makes these novels so convincing is their
human and mundane quality. There may be war in
heaven or descent into hell, but always the focus of
action is on earth with real people who have real
problems, whether it be in an English village, or in a
London office, in a pub or a villa. This practical,
earthly concern prevents Williams' books from becoming sheer fantasy. We can identify ourselves with
at least some of the characters and with them move
through a series of experiences that may enlighten and
ennoble our present life.

In this century Williams has no peer in the field of
Christian allegory. The subtlety of his characterizations, the wide breadth of his scenes, the control and
beauty of his language, the complexity, inventiveness
and variety of his plots, the vivid imagery, and the
depth of his thought support my claim. He has few
rivals in this field and may rank with Bunyan and
Spenser as a craftsman of the highest order. His novels
give clear evidence of this author's rare combination
of talents and of his astounding energy, enthusiasm,
zest for life, and remarkable literary skills. We have
reason, therefore, to lament his untimely death.

ROSE MACAULAY

William J. Lockwood

DAME ROSE MACAULAY (*ca.* 1889–1958), the daughter
of G. C. Macaulay, a Cambridge don, was born into a
large family in a university atmosphere. On account of
the illness of the mother, the family moved to an
Italian town on the coast where Rose spent her entire
childhood, except for occasional visits to England. She
returned to London to attend preparatory school and
later entered Oxford. Soon after her first book, *Abbots
Verney*, in 1906, she began to come up to London,
and after a time, her uncle gave her a flat off Chancery
Lane. In London she entered literary society and became acquainted with Edith Sitwell, Walter de la
Mare, and Aldous Huxley among others. Rupert
Brooke, a close friend, took her around. She, in turn,
later introduced a new female novelist, Elizabeth
Bowen, to London and treated her with great kindness.

Near the center of the literary world during a color-
ful and crucial transitional period in modern British
literature, Rose Macaulay is an interesting, curious
figure. This child of the Edwardian world, more than
usually removed from the mainstream of life, arrived
in London with a brave and determinedly cleareyed
manner. One of the chief interests of her work, therefore, is her honest representation of the shock of that
experience as projected in the lives of her heroes and
heroines. Her vision, which in her early novels shares

the searching, prewar earnestness of E. M. Forster, veers in the direction of Huxley, Ford Madox Ford, and T. S. Eliot. It becomes a vision of a civilization, under the stress of World War I, going to pieces. With it, of course, go the world's moral bearings, and the problem of Faith, taken up by Eliot and others, becomes of central importance.

It will be seen from these remarks that Rose Macaulay is a minor novelist not because of the eccentric nature of her materials, but because of the fact that she is limited in her ability to handle them. The range of her vision is confined to the upper middle-class, Anglican-Cambridge stratum of society, even though she tries to work beyond that range. Also, she is limited in her ability to deal with the disturbing, personal repercussions of the world she represents. Indeed, it almost seems that she knew she was going beyond herself in her choice of materials, and in trying to face up to the job, developed a no-nonsense, oversimplified and often, therefore, artificial manner of representation.

But admitting these limitations, and they are severe in too much of her writing, she *has* won a distinct identity in modern British literary history; we recognize a voice that is uniquely Rose Macaulay.

One first notices that voice in *The Lee Shore* (1912). Not a great novel in itself, it is worth reading for two reasons. First, we can see in it elements that recur in the novels, certain images and themes defining the pattern that eventually emerges from her writings. Secondly, this novel is worth reading because in it we find a novelist without the defenses of sophistication that she later finds in the satiric novels, a writer solemn and almost naked in her earnestness. And it is out of this vulnerable, inner self that, much later, following the long drought in her creativity between 1934 and 1955, renewal comes in *The Towers of Trebizond*.

The title, *The Lee Shore*, suggests its hero's abandonment of the world and his drift toward a place of refuge from it. At the same time, this image reflects the poetic quality of this novel, one that becomes dominant at the end and ultimately defines the hero's quest for and achievement of personal salvation.

The hero's salvation is awarded by default. It follows from loss, from the failure of human relationships. One aspect of a complex set of human relationships depicted in this novel is the triangle that forms when Dennis, the older half-brother of the unlucky hero, Peter Margierson, marries. It is actually a submerged love triangle, for Dennis' bride, Lucy, is the young woman with whom Peter had enjoyed a warm friendship and an unexpressed love. Peter, moreover, has admired and loved Dennis. The story that follows is one of painful estrangement. As the wife of the successful Dennis Urqhart, and thereby one of the respectable family of Urqharts, Lucy finds herself in the world of the "Haves." Peter, on the other hand, after marrying (out of pity) an English orphan girl named Rhoda, and after losing his job as agent for a wealthy art collector, finds himself among the "Have-nots."

A second story of friendship, estrangement, and failure is the story of Peter and Rhoda's relationship with Peter's step-brother, Hilary, and his wife, Peggy. Staking the remains of his savings on an English boarding house scheme, Peter leaves Italy in order to support himself and the jobless Hilary; and it is then that his misfortunes begin. After giving birth to a boy, Peter's wife runs off with a former lover; the tenants start to move out; finally, when Peter gets ill, Hilary decides, against the protests of the generous-hearted Peggy, to desert him and his child and go off to seek his fortune in Dublin.

The crisis of the novel coincides with the breaking away from human relationships and the subsequent drift to the "lee shore," the out-of-the-way Italian coastal town Peter and his son ultimately find. The crisis is precipitated soon after Hilary's departure by the chance meeting between Lucy and Peter. At this point in the novel, Peter's increasing tendency to give up the struggle is momentarily reversed. His love re-kindled, he decides he must have Lucy. They will for once seize life together and damn the consequences. Leaving friendship and civilization behind, they will know only "the primitive, selfish, human love that demands body and soul."

But though the writer is here momentarily carried away with the Forsterian idea of resurrecting Pan in a world of overcivilized, underdeveloped hearts, Rose Macaulay ultimately *is* on the side of civilization, of the forces of order as against the powers of darkness and moral chaos. Consequently, in the next chapter we find our protagonist convinced of the irresponsibility and impossibility of his plan. Not only does his old love for Dennis make it wrong in his own eyes. He would also be deserting his lot in life, which is, he comes to realize, not with those who seize, but those who suffer, "who drop all cargoes . . . overboard . . . and when they're driven by the winds at last onto a lee shore . . . find on the shore colored shells to play with and still are gay" (p. 279). And so we return to the dominant theme-image of the lee shore that runs throughout the novel. It was first projected out of Peter's state of feeling following the news of his wife's flight.

> For the first time he was seeing the world not as a glorious treasure-place full of glad things for touch and sight and hearing, full of delightful people and absurd jokes, but as a grey and lonely sea through which one drifted rudderless towards a lee shore. He supposed that there was, somewhere, a lee shore; a place where the winds, having blown their uttermost, ceased to blow, and where wrecked things were cast up at last broken beyond all mending and beyond all struggling, to find the peace of the utterly lost.—(p. 248)

And the image returns again, impressively, at the novel's end.

One of the chief pleasures of this novel is Rose Macaulay's lee shore landscapes. The opening lines of the last chapter, "On the Shore," project a vision of fruitfulness and serenity that is sustained through the end.

> There is a shore along which the world flowers, one long sweet garden strip, between olive-grey hills and the very blue sea. Like nosegays in the garden the towns are set, blooming in their many colours, linked by the white road running along blue water. For vagabonds in April the poppies riot scarlet by the white road's edge, and the last of the hawthorne lingers like melting snow, and over the garden walls the purple veils of the wistaria drift like twilight mist. Over the garden walls, too, the sweetness of the orange and lemon blossom floats into the road, and the frangipani sends delicate wafts down, and the red and white roses toss and hang as if they brimmed over from sheer exuberance.
>
> . . . .
>
> The road itself is good, bordered on one side by the garden sweetness and the blossoms that foam like wave-crests over the walls, on the other breaking down to a steep hill-slope where all the wild flowers of spring star the grassy terraces, singing at the twisted feet of the olives that give them grey shadow.—(p. 284)

This vision of sea, flowers, and fruit recurs throughout Rose Macaulay's writings and is beautifully consummated in her last novel, *The Towers of Trebizond* (1956), when its full significance is realized. Ultimately, as I think we shall see, Rose Macaulay's real kinship is with a world beyond human relationships.

Unfortunately, however, the transcendent, lyrical beauty of the novel's end does not undo the author's failure to fill in this complexly designed, at times impressively poetic, novel with real flesh and blood. She asserts suffering but does not convey it as a living reality. For example, her handling of what is, structurally, the crucial Lucy-Peter scene in the novel is completely inadequate. The whole situation seems absurdly artificial, especially when Peter, responding to

Lucy's offer to run off to Italy with him (and his child), cries,

> "Oh d'you mean it Lucy? D'you mean you'll come and play with us, for ever and ever?"
> "Course I will," she said, simply, like a child.

A related weakness in this novel, as in the following, *Views and Vagabonds*, is Miss Macaulay's handling of the lower classes. Her representation of the "Have-nots" is mannered, sentimental, and faintly condescending (though not meant to be so). At times her naïveté is embarrassing, as when, for example, she talks very seriously about Lucy's true identification with all the "down-below" people: "You understand them and they understand you . . . Dennis and his friends and the servants and everyone thinks it's idiotic to be a vegetarian." Perhaps the author is letting Lucy's words betray her innermost character here, for Lucy does ultimately stay on with Dennis (charity begins at home with the "Haves"), but this tone is hardly distinguishable from Rose Macaulay's manner throughout the novel as, to give another example, when Peter describes among the beggars "a man all done up in bandages, hopping on crutches and grinning. Smashed to bits, and his bones sticking out of his skin for hunger . . . saying *nihil habentes, omnia possidentes;* isn't it a jolly day?" It is of interest, too, to note that most of her down-below people, both in *The Lee Shore* and *Views and Vagabonds* are not the English poor but exotic types—mainly Italians or gypsies, more often than not somehow connected with the bohemian life.

In *Views and Vagabonds* (1912) we find another suffering antihero in Benjie. Even more principle-conscious than Peter, Benjie renounces his middle-class identity (notably represented in the personages of Lord and Lady Bunter) and embraces socialism. At first, believing in the dignity of the man who works with his hands, he becomes a blacksmith. Later, carrying on the William Morris mission, he journeys round the countryside trying to convince workingmen to buy, at small cost, the useful and beautiful household objects he has fashioned, in order to emancipate their households from ugliness.

But Benjie's idealism is misunderstood. People don't like to be told that their furniture and their pictures are ugly, and Benjie is jeered, abused, and run out of one town after another. In the last town he visits he is mobbed and beaten unconscious, emerging near the end of the novel as a bloodstained, Christlike figure, suffering for the sins of mankind.

By way of contrast with Benjie, Miss Macaulay offers in the Crevequers a vision of selfish, pagan joyfulness. An Italian gypsy family and the vagabonds of the novel's title, they sponge without conscience in times of need, and share without restraint or discrimination in time of prosperity. These simple, Pan-like figures undermine Benjie's belief in honest toil and so bear the brunt of his cold disapproval through most of the novel. But in the course of being nursed back to health by the Crevequers, Benjie finally recognizes his love for them and discovers his true kinship with them. They offer gaiety in despair, a reassertion of the need to enjoy the simple pleasures of life as they come. The resolution is similar to that of *The Lee Shore*, but it seems more contrived because of the obviously conceptual nature of the opposed views. The author seems to be trying too hard to write an E. M. Forsterian novel.

Views and Vagabonds looks forward to *Potterism* and the novels of the twenties. There are more ideas here—Fabianism and free love for example—that represent the drift of the times. Moreover, the cynical figures of Anne Vickery and Hugh Bunter, and the representation of the absurdly committed Cecil, point to a new interest in detachment. The attractive, mocking personality of Anne Vickery in this novel resembles Katherine Varick, Nan, and Rome Garden of

Potterism, Dangerous Ages, and *Told by an Idiot* and suggests the cool tone and ironic point of view that Miss Macaulay is on her way to discovering.

In *Potterism* (1920) the Urqharts and the Bunters of the world are properly put on the defensive. A new hardheaded breed of clear-thinking, nonsentimental young people displace the vulnerable and suffering idealists of the earlier novels. A far wiser lot, they are committed to nothing more than seeing things *as they are.*

The dedication Miss Macaulay prefixes to this novel identifies her purpose, and the technique she employs admirably suits that purpose. The novel is dedicated

To the
Unsentimental Precisians in Thought,
Who Have, on this Confused,
Inaccurate, and Emotional Planet,
no Fit Habitation

In this spirit the unsentimental, precise, and thoughtful author presents her materials in an objective fashion. The novel is divided into six parts. The author objectifies herself as R. M., the third person narrator of Parts I and VI which provide a framework for the novel. The material within that framework consists of a sequence of four juxtaposed monologues.

The juxtaposition of Parts II and III dramatizes the central tension in the novel. Part III is told by Leila Yorke, the pen name of a sentimental and platitudinous female novelist of the late Victorian variety, whose real name is Mrs. Potter. She is the wife of the man who, as head of the major publishing syndicate in England, is the virtual voice of the middle class. Part II is told by Gideon, a Russian Jew of an Anglicized, upper-middle class family, who edits an antipotterite weekly review, appropriately named the

Weekly Fact. The product of one of those "unsentimental precisians of thought" who are resisting the
dangerous muddling efforts of their middle-class
world, the *Weekly Fact* tells the undistorted truth—
without sentimentality and without platitudes.

The tale "Told by Gideon" begins its account of
1919, the opening year of this section of the narrative,
with these words: "It was a queer, inconclusive, lazy,
muddled, reckless, unsatisfactory, rather ludicrous
time." The December elections, the religious up-
heaval, Labour, and the International were among the
issues muddled by the Potter Press. By the time you'd
read a leader on the subject of the miner's strike, for
example, says Gideon,

> You'd have got the impression that the strikers were
> Bolshevists helped by German money and aiming at a
> social revolution, instead of discontented, needy, and
> greedy British workmen, grabbing at more money and
> less work, in the normal, greedy, human way we all have.
> —(p. 78)

By contrast with the precise, cool, objective tone of
this passage, Part III, "Told by Leila Yorke," begins

> Love and truth are the only things that count. I have
> often thought that they are like two rafts on the stormy
> sea of life. . . . If we follow these two stars patiently,
> they will guide us at last into port.

Gideon and Mrs. Potter come into conflict because
of his close relationship with her daughter, Jane Potter. Of the bright and clever new generation, and
herself an anti-Potterite, Jane gets a job working for
the *Weekly Fact*. The friendship that forms between
herself and Gideon grows into love. But distrusting
sentimentality and too much emphasis on the matter
of sex, their love remains unspoken. Before it does get
spoken, Oliver Hobart, a handsome potterite comes
along and Jane falls in love and marries him. Against
the deepest wishes of her husband, Jane continues in
her job on the *Fact* and expects her friendship with

Gideon to remain unchanged. But, on one occasion, finding her at the flat of Katherine Varick, a common friend, Gideon takes her home. "And here," Gideon writes, "if any one wants to know why I regard 'being in love' as a disastrous kink in the mental machinery, is the reason. It impels you to do things against all your reasoned will and intentions." Against his will, he speaks her name and discovers the love he had never admitted to himself.

When in the next moment, they become aware of Jane's husband standing in the doorway, the scene is set for what Rose Macaulay calls a "Potter melodrama." Yawning, Jane contemptuously dismisses the scene and goes off to her room. Oliver then insinuates, when Gideon presses him, what he is not brave enough to say outright, and the situation ends on a note of awkward hostility. But this is not the end of things, for the next event in the novel is the death of Oliver. He has either fallen, or been pushed, down the stairs.

At this point in the narrative, the Gideon-Leila Yorke (Mrs. Potter) tension comes to the surface. Out of revenge for his hold over her daughter, Leila Yorke invents the suspicion, blown up in the Potter press, that Gideon had murdered Oliver after the scene in the apartment. When it turns out, however, that it was actually Jane's sister Clare—it was she who had first fallen in love with Oliver—who had pushed Oliver to his death, Truth, one of those twin guiding stars in the sea of life, is quickly blotted out. The Potter Press drops its innuendo and demand for an investigation and from beneath the mask of Leila Yorke the real Mrs. Potter, whose true voice had been heard in the concluding paragraph of Part III, comes to the surface. She had concluded her narrative with the comment, "I couldn't help wondering how it would affect the *Weekly Fact* if its editor were to be arrested on a charge of wilful murder" (p. 124).

As one nears the end of the novel, the voice of

R. M., uncommitted at the beginning, becomes identified with the voice of Gideon. From the web of late Victorian hypocrisy and complacency, he emerges as the hero of the novel. But it is of that antiheroic kind one comes to expect in Rose Macaulay. Though he and Jane declare their love and decide to marry, the love story has a tragic ending. Because she is pregnant with a child by Oliver the marriage has to be delayed, and before they do marry Gideon is killed, during a visit to Russia, by a band of fanatic Bolshevists.

Side by side in this novel, Miss Macaulay presents a satiric attack on the Potters of the world and, in the Gideon story, a vision of futility. Essentially they are of the same stuff for the one is ultimately ineffective and the latter simply leads R. M. back to a deepened sense of the necessity of noncommitment in an absurd universe.

> Sentimentalism spread a rosy veil over the ugliness, draping it decently. Making it, thought Gideon, how much worse; but making it such as Potterites could face unwincing.
> The rain beat down. At its soft, chill touch Gideon's brain cooled and cooled, till he seemed to see everything in a cold, hard, crystal clarity. Life and death — how little they mattered. Life was paltry, and death its end. — (p. 203)

The cynical, noncommitted position suggested here affords Rose Macaulay a discriminating yet inclusive point of view. The fine balance she strikes between the two in *Potterism* accounts for the consistency of tone and the overall success of this novel. But the R. M. of Part VI is skating on thin ice. Just below the surface of her narrative is a pessimism that merges into despair. The strong suicidal note which runs through Rose Macaulay's next novel, *Dangerous Ages*, is a manifestation of loss of proportion, the great danger besetting the cynic's precise but brittle technique. Likewise, in this period of her writing, all manifestations of sentimentality are suspect. But there is a point beyond which such an attitude becomes limiting; and it must be admitted that one of Rose Macaulay's major limitations as a novelist is her distrust of natural feeling. At first sight, the following words of Gideon are refreshing in their clearheadedness; on second sight they are somehow sterile.

> We [he and Jane] couldn't go on. It was too second-rate. It was anti-social, stupid, uncivilised, all I most hated, to let emotion play the devil. . . .
>
> Now there are some loves that the world, important though it is, may be well lost for—the love of an idea, a principle, a cause . . . but. . . . I hate the whole tribe of sentimental men and women who, impelled by the imaginative fool nature, exalt sexual love above its proper place in the scheme of things.—(p. 85)

One wonders, what with all the aborted love relationships in her novels due to the accidental death of the lover involved, whether her attack on sentimentality is not defensive, a reaction to the expression of natural human feeling—especially between the sexes and in particular of a sexual nature—which basically frightens her. The recurrent motif (almost a preoccupation) concerning the relative freedom of women, specifically their freedom from motherhood, may, apart from the fact that it was an issue of the times, be related to this fear. And the inadequacy of the Peter-Lucy love scene again comes to mind.

Of the three novels in this major phase of Rose Macaulay's career *Dangerous Ages* is least good. It is structurally deficient; no very coherent reflection of human experience is achieved by the time one comes to the closing pages. But there are some unfused elements, very good in themselves, that anticipate her impressive *Told by an Idiot*.

One of these elements, the recurrent image of seaweed, passively drifting with the tide and being tossed about in the waves, looks both backward and forward. It recalls the poetic quality of *The Lee Shore*, while at the same time, in that crucial scene wherein a group

of persons are very nearly swept out to sea and
drowned, it is a darker, more despairing image. No
promise of a lee shore comes out of this visualization.
The poetry is derived from danger, a brush with
death, and this is the kind of concentration and intensity one feels in viewing the smashup of civilization at
the end of *Told by an Idiot*.

In *Dangerous Ages* the sea does have a peace-giving
power, of course. If nothing else it can, in making one
aware of the vanity of life, reinforce one's resistance to
worldliness. Thus Nan, the middle-aged woman entering her forties, who may I suppose be regarded as the
novel's heroine, finds comfort in the sound of the sea.
The incident comes at the painful point in the novel
when Barry Briscoe, with whom she has had an affair
and with whom she is still in love, is falling in love
with her youthful niece, Gerda. "The waves beat now;
ran up whisperingly with the incoming tide, broke,
and sidled back, dragging at the wet sand. . . . Nan,
hearing them, drifted at last into sleep" (p. 144). In
the same way, Imogen in *Told by an idiot* is to find an
anodyne in the routine of war office work, a numbing
of the pain of having lost, in the war, first her lover
and then her brother.

The deepening of Rose Macaulay's cynicism in this
crucial period of the twenties is evident. It manifests
itself in the loss of the poetic, seascape image in *Told
by an Idiot* and in the consequent shift toward a dry,
almost purely intellectual plane. And it may be
plotted in the change of setting in these three novels:
from Soho and Picadilly Circus in *Potterism* to Nan's
retreat to an out-of-the-way seacoast town in *Dangerous Ages* to Rome Garden's drawing room in *Told by
an Idiot*.

The scenes set at Polperro, the seacoast town in
Dangerous Ages, mark the turning point in this stage
of Rose Macaulay's career. Nan's cycling down twist-
ing roads on the edge of ocean precipices is thrilling,
but this impatience of hers for "vehement living" is

suicidal. In the same way, descriptions of the Polperro landscape offer moments of joy and lyrical beauty in the novel, but even this pleasure is too intense to be sustained: "Polperro had the eerie beauty of a dream or of a little foreign port. Such beauty and charm are on the edge of pain; you cannot disentangle them from it. They intoxicate, and pierce to tears" — (p. 162).

Told by an Idiot (1923) offers the reader one of the author's most attractive heroines in Rome Garden. Her vision of the world is taken from that moment in *Macbeth* that supplies both Rose Macaulay and William Faulkner a title: "Life's but a walking shadow . . . it is a tale / Told by an idiot, full of sound and fury, / Signifying nothing." Admitting this vision of nonsignificance, Rose Macaulay is nevertheless able to identify with Rome Garden's enjoyment of "the cheering spectacle of human absurdity." Beautiful and cynical, Rome Garden is an eighteenth-century figure, akin to Voltaire — cleareyed, mocking, and gay.

The point of view implicit in a splendid scene in *Dangerous Ages* is taken up in this novel and sustained. In that scene Miss Macaulay renders the reluctant visit of Mrs. Hilary with Rosalind, a langorously beautiful and morally relaxed young woman whom her son plans to marry. The occasion is tea, and the setting Rosalind's rather voluptuously furnished drawing room. The pleasure to be derived from this scene is in the writer's control of the comic situation, an awareness of the incongruity of manners she perceives in this Victorian mother's embarrassed visit with this distinctly modern, and for her, incomprehensible woman. Seeing Mrs. Hilary's emotional fuss over the welfare of her son as a lost cause, or at any rate an unnecessary one in an altered world, Miss Macaulay adopts a point of view which resembles Rome Garden's in *Told by an Idiot* wherein Rome is described as a "slight, pale, delicate young woman, with ironic green eyes and mocking lips a little compressed at the corners."

Rome Garden's position as observer of the passing spectacle is made clear from the beginning. In the section entitled "Fin-De-Siècle," the narrator tells us that in 1890 people called her "intensely modern," and yet, she maintains, the Rome Gardens have existed in every age.

> In 1790, 1690, 1590, and back through every decade of every century, there have been Rome Gardens, fastidious, *mondaine*, urbane, lettered, critical, amused, sceptical and what was called in 1890 *fin-de-siècle*. It is not a type which, so to speak, makes the world go round; it does not assist movements nor join crusades; it coolly distrusts enthusiasm and eschews the heat and ardour of the day. It is to be found among both sexes equally, and is the stuff of which the urbane bachelor and spinster, rather than the spouse and parent, are made.— (pp. 78–79)

Much of the pleasure of this novel comes from the spectacle of the passing show, the procession of recent western civilization. The periods leading to its debacle provide the chief structural device of the novel. Parts I, II, III, and IV are entitled "Victorian," "Fin-De-Siècle," "Edwardian," and "Georgian," the latter being further subdivided into periods titled "Circus," "Smash," and "Debris" (prewar, war, and postwar through the early twenties). Those interested in the transition between the nineteenth- and twentieth-century worlds will derive a peculiar pleasure from her evocation of the Edwardian period, especially her characterization of King Edward as an early modern.

> There was nothing dowdy about our King Edward. He set the stakes high, and all who could afford it played. Pageants and processions passed in regal splendour. . . .
> Ideals changed . . . No more were unfortunate ladies who had had marital troubles coldly banned from court, for a larger charity (except as to suits, dinners and wall-papers) obtained.—(pp. 199–200)

Of like interest is her evocation of the end of the first
phase of the Georgian period, 1910–14.

> Rome was a happy Georgian. . . .
>   So the Cheerful spectacle of a world of fools bright-
> ened Rome's afternoon years. Before long, the folly was
> to become too desperate, too disastrous, too wrecking a
> business to be a comic show even to the most amused
> eyes; the circus was, all too soon, to go smash, and the
> folly of the clowns who had helped to smash it became
> a bitterness, and the idiot's tale held too much of sound
> and fury to be borne. But these first Georgian years
> were to Rome twinkling with bland absurdity.—(pp.
> 286–87)

A shift in tone, from the gaiety of the circus spectacle to the grotesque fantasy of a world going to
pieces, may be observed as one nears the end of this
tale. With its approach and the coming of World
War I the tempo of the novel becomes desperate in its
ironic juxtapositions of Imogen's fantasies about life
on a fruit-laden Pacific isle and the coming cataclysm.
The fact that Rose Macaulay skips over the years
1914–18 and describes them only in retrospect may be
held against her. Whether she does this out of a sense
of her own limitations as a writer or out of her inabil-
ity to face up to some of the more disturbing realities
of the twentieth-century world is difficult to say with
assurance—most probably, both. Perhaps it is unkind
to find a correspondence between her avoidance of the
war in this novel (as in all her novels) and her failure
in handling love relationships. But once again the love
relationship between Rome Garden and her lover,
Mr. Jayne, is aborted by his violent, accidental death.
It is in harmony with the dark, cataclysmic vision she
presents in this novel, but there is, fundamentally, a
certain fear of the animal-man, whether at love or at
war.

One final aspect of *Told by an Idiot* needs to be
discussed, and that concerns the author's technique.

The success of the novels in this period owes much to the fact that Rose Macaulay finds a voice suited to her, one of coolness and detachment that gives her writing a consistency of tone and of point of view. The technique that suits this purpose is chiefly one of juxtaposition whose effect is ironic, humorous, mocking. As a means toward seeing things objectively, as they are, this is an impressive form and works consistently well in *Potterism*. But to fix on the shattered pieces of life and to ignore the life principle is to court despair. Moreover, there is the danger of method becoming mannerism, a way of seeing that becomes constrictive, and ultimately fixed and sterile. *Told by an Idiot* can be squeezed out in 1923, and then her creative impulse dries up for thirty-three years.

After *Told by an Idiot* Rose Macaulay veers away from serious treatments of her subject. She attempts to revive the humor of *Potterism* and turn it into comedy. Her most nearly successful attempt is *Orphan Island* (1924), a satiric, utopian novel. A group of Englishmen, shipwrecked on a desert island, procreate and build a civilized little world resembling late nineteenth-century England. The stranded Mrs. Smith, mother and matriarch of the island family, is a Queen Victoria figure. Social and religious absurdities of Victorian England are represented and laughed about. But Miss Macaulay's talents have rather dried up and her dependence upon old materials is obvious. There is little imagination in the working out of this interesting idea.

But there is even less in the other seven novels she writes in this period, most of them also using Potterite themes and techniques. Thus Denham, in *Crewe Train* (1926), a reworking of Imogen in *Told by an Idiot*, is a creature of animal spirit who goes to London but refuses to be civilized. Aside from the idea itself, which has possibilities, there is little of interest in this static and poorly structured novel. There is an increase of missionaries (chiefly eccentric Anglican ones) but her treatment of them is dry and unless one enjoys Church jokes they are a pretty dull lot.

Miss Macaulay turns during this period in the direction of nonfiction. *They Were Defeated* (1932), for example, is a historical novel. It comes out of her interest in the seventeenth century which produced between 1931 and 1935 the scholarly *Some Religious Elements in English Literature,* an anthology titled *Minor Pleasures of Life,* and a biography, *Milton.* Its only connection with her earlier fiction is its Cambridge setting and its concern with religion.

Wit combined with fantasy or with narrative romps characterize *Keeping Up Appearances* (1928), *Staying with Relations* (1930) and *Going Abroad* (1934). Of these *Going Abroad* is most interesting because of the presence of certain elements she later uses in *The Towers of Trebizond.* Chiefly, there is the vital Mrs. Aubrey who has just come from Mesopotamia where her clergyman husband has been seeking out the site of the Garden of Eden. Her own theory is that Eden is located somewhere in the Basque country, the picturesque background of this novel. The descriptions of the Basque landscape—Rose Macaulay's love of exotic fruits remains—are quite good in themselves; they foreshadow those of the more strange and more beautiful shores of the Black Sea in *The Towers of Trebizond.*

In *The Towers of Trebizond* (1956), Rose Macaulay discovers a new voice. It is not the cool, detached voice of an agreeable *persona* as in the novels of the twenties, but is the personal voice of her own, hitherto submerged, personality. It is heard in the amusing scenes and episodes that abound in the novel. Standing near the sad ruins of that spot near the Black Sea where Troy was believed to have stood, Aunt Dot says she thought the city ought to be dug up and reconstructed. "But I thought there were enough cities standing about the world already, and that those which had disappeared had better be let alone, lying under the grass and asphodel and brambles, with the wind sighing over them" (p. 30). Later, describing the range of humanity on board the Trabzon, a Turkish ship bound from Istanbul for Trebizond, Miss Macaulay offers this deft, tongue-in-cheek rendering of a *mélange* of cultures, a curious, mid-century scene.

> We all thought it was very admirable in the male Turks to meet for worship so regularly when voyaging; Christian travellers are seldom seen to do this, unless they are pilgrims. But Father Chantry-Pigg set up his portable altar in a corner of the upper deck were it could be seen from the steerage deck and said Mass before it each morning, and aunt Dot and Dr. Halide and I attended, and we were watched by the Turks on the steerage deck and sailors and bar waiters and passengers, among whom were two American girls in bikinis sun bathing, and more Turks watched the American girls than us.— (pp. 51–52)

As will be noted in these passages, her style is more gentle, less affected, and funnier. Also, the lyrical, first person narration gives a warmth and a consistency of tone and point of view, qualities lacking in many of her earlier novels.

The real magic of this novel is the ease and naturalness with which it appears to have been constructed. Once the central unifying image was conceived and understood, the design and the words seem simply to have followed it through. Trebizond, cite of the splendid, ancient Byzantine city on the shores of the Pontine, comes to be identified with the heroine Laurie's frustrating, lifelong quest for some lost core of meaningfulness. "The last Greek empire brooded like a ghost in that forlorn fag end of time to which I too had come, lost and looking for I did not know what" (pp. 145–46). As the symbol of a lost past, it is a projection of Rose Macaulay's own attempt to reconcile her Christian tradition with a faithless world of which she finds herself a part.

One of the wonderful moments in the novel is Laurie's dream of the past ages of Trebizond, a strange and beautiful vision induced by the green potion she gets from a Comus-like enchanter. Another is her dream of Jason and the Argonauts, and their quest upon the strange waters of the Black Sea, a symbol of her own spiritual voyaging. Most moving, however, is Laurie's vision of the shining towers of Trebizond which figure the New Jerusalem, the City of God on earth. Beautiful and terrible at the same time, it is a projection of that which she seeks and yet despairs of achieving.

> Still the towers of Trebizond, the fabled city, shimmer on a far horizon, gated and walled and held in a luminous enchantment. It seems that for me, and however much I must stand outside them, this must for ever be. But at the city's heart lie the pattern and the hard core, and these I can never make my own: they are too far outside my range. The pattern should perhaps be easier, the core less hard. — (pp. 276–77)

On the narrative level, the ambivalence of this symbol is a projection of the heroine's internal conflict between her love for Vere and her love for God. As one might expect in a Rose Macaulay novel, the heroine meets her lover, Vere, and after a beautiful week of love in Venice he is killed in a car crash. But there is something more here. For one thing, it is because of her own impulsiveness that the accident occurs. For another, the death of the lover is not the end of things, but the point of departure, on the part of the heroine, for a full, truthful introspection. Seeing the facts without sentimentality does not here become an excuse for avoiding Laurie's conflict between her natural feelings and her awareness of the wrongfulness of her relationship with a man married to another woman. What is impressive here is not only the clear-mindedness but the emotional honesty with which the heroine is endowed. Before Vere's death she speaks thus of her relationship with him.

> I did not really want to be saved from my sins, not for the time being, it would make things too difficult and too sad. I was getting into a stage when I was not quite sure what sin was, I was in a kind of fog . . . a confused sort of twilight in which everything is blurred, and the next thing you know you might be stealing or anything, because right and wrong have become things you do not look at . . . and it seems better to live in a blur. Then come the times when you wake suddenly up.
> —(p. 150)

After his death, she says:

> Someone once said that hell would be, and now is, living without God and with evil, and being unable to get used to it. . . . I live now in two hells, for I have lost God and live also without love, or without the love I want, and I cannot get used to that either.—(pp. 275–76)

In the Trebizond symbol Rose Macaulay has achieved a strong and beautiful resolution of the conflicting tendencies in her real and in her fictional personality. She has struck a note of concord and mellowness in her lifelong love-hate relationship with the modern world, neither reacting against it nor submitting to it, but treating it with generous humor. In the same way, she has settled her relationship with the Anglican Church. Setting its achievements off against its failures, Laurie concedes its moments of magnificence and courage.

> And this failure of the Christian Church . . . is one of the saddest things that has happened in all the world. But it is what happens when a magnificent idea has to be worked out by human beings who do not understand much of it but interpret it in their own way and think they are guided by God, whom they have not yet grasped. And yet they had grasped something, so that the Church . . . has flowered up in learning and cul-

ture and beauty and art, to set against its darkness and incivility . . . and I, at least, want to be inside it.— (pp. 196–97)

This mood of resolution leaves Rose Macaulay, now Dame Macaulay, free to indulge her taste for the pleasures of life. The novel's rhythms are guided by moods alternately *l'allegro* and *il penseroso*. On the one hand, there are rich descriptions of fruit and fish: "I knew as well that Trebizond held something for me, and it was there that I might try to sort out my own problems too, in the derelict forlorn grandeur of that fallen Greek empire with its ghosts, and its rich sweet fruits, especially figs, and its sea full of the most exotic fish." (p. 132) On the other hand, it is filled with the delicious sadness of a landscape belonging to a lost world. "All the centuries of lively Byzantine chatter, they had left whispering echoes in that place where the hot sun beat down on the fig trees and the small wind and small animals stirred in the long grass."—(p. 145)

Hoyt—Robert Smith Surtees

1. Introduction to Byron's *Don Juan* (New York, 1949), p. viii.
2. Quoted by E. D. Cuming, *Robert Smith Surtees* (New York, 1924), p. 308.
3. It is necessary to distinguish between the "Old Sporting" and the "New Sporting," which Surtees himself founded in 1831. They ran simultaneously.
4. This is E. D. Cuming, who edited and extended Surtees' autobiographical remains in *Robert Smith Surtees*.
5. Cuming, p. 75.
6. Cuming, p. 132.
7. For bibliographical material I am principally indebted to Ralph Nevill's *Old English Sporting Books* (London, 1924), itself a collector's item.
8. Quoted by Cuming, p. 245.

McCabe—Benjamin Disraeli

1. All quotations are from the *Bradenham Edition of the Novels and Tales of Benjamin Disraeli, 1st Earl of Beaconsfield*, 12 vols. (New York, 1926–27). Volume, chapter, and page references are given.

Nash—Arthur Machen Among the Arthurians

1. Nathan Comfort Starr, *King Arthur Today* (Gainesville, Florida, 1954). A discussion of modern reworkings of the Arthurian material.

2. One of the recent studies of Machen (Reynolds and Charlton's *Arthur Machen*) suggests a division of several of the tales into *pièces roses* and *pièces noires*.

3. Arthur Machen, "The White Powder," *The Three Imposters* (New York, 1930), p. 183.

4. *Ibid.*, pp. 190–91.

5. Arthur Machen, *Tales of Horror and the Supernatural* with an introduction by Philip Van Doren Stern (London, 1949), p. 182.

6. *Ibid.*, p. 114.

7. *Ibid.*, p. 426.

8. *Ibid.*, pp. 110–11.

9. Edgar Allan Poe, *Tales of Mystery and Imagination* (New York, 1933), p. 382.

10. Aidan Reynolds and William Charlton, *Arthur Machen* (London, 1963), p. 50.

11. *The Three Imposters*, pp. 118–26.

12. *Tales of Horror and the Supernatural*, p. 206.

13. *Ibid.*, p. 154.

14. *Ibid.*, p. 239.

15. *Ibid.*, p. 243.

16. *Ibid.*, p. 242.

Wandall—Charles Williams

1. C. S. Lewis, T. S. Eliot, Dorothy Sayers, J. K. Tolkein, and others.

2. Elizabeth Drew, *T. S. Eliot: The Design of His Poetry* (New York, 1950), p. 3.

3. *Ibid.*, p. 18.

4. Fred B. Millett, *Reading Fiction* (New York, 1950), pp. 53–55.

5. Charles Williams, *Judgement at Chelmsford*, a pageant play, 1939. Williams wrote this play using the pseudonym "Peter Stanhope."

6. For definitions of secularization and secularism, see Harvey Cox, *The Secular City* (New York, 1965), p. 20.

7. D. G. James, *Scepticism and Poetry* (London, 1937), p. 271.